Letters to Harry

Letters to Harry

The *true* story of a daughter's love
and a mother's final journey

JANET FARRINGTON GRAHAM

Time-Life Books is a division of Time Life Inc.

TIME LIFE INC.
President and CEO George Artandi

TIME-LIFE CUSTOM PUBLISHING
Vice President and Publisher Terry Newell
Vice President of Sales and Marketing Neil Levin
Director of Creative Services Laura Ciccone McNeill
Director of Special Markets Liz Ziehl
Project Manager Jennie Halfant
Production Manager Carolyn Clark
Quality Assurance Manager James D. King

EDITORIAL STAFF FOR *LETTERS TO HARRY*
Design Red Herring Design/NYC
Special Contributors Celia Beattie, Nancy Burke, Louise Collazo
Jacket photo © M. Gesinger/Photonica
Pictures on pages 11 and 97: © PhotoDisc.

First printing. Printed in U.S.A.
Pre-Press Services Time-Life Imaging Center

TIME-LIFE is a trademark of Time Warner Inc. U.S.A.

LIBRARY OF CONGRESS CATALOGING-IN-PUBLICATION DATA
Graham, Janet Farrington, 1955-
Letters to Harry : a true story of a daughter's love and a
mother's final journey / Janet Farrington Graham.
p. cm.
ISBN 0-7370-0046-5
1. Breast--Cancer. 2. Graham, Janet Farrington, 1955---Correspondence. 3. Mothers and daughters. I. Title.
RC280.B8 G697 1999
362.1'9699449'0092--dc21
[B]
98-3221
CIP

Books produced by Time-Life Custom Publishing are available at a special bulk discount for promotional and premium use. Custom adaptations can also be created to meet your specific marketing goals. Call 1-800-323-5255.

For my father

[CONTENTS]

[INTRODUCTION]

*E*very word of this book is the truth as I know it; every letter was sent the day it was dated. And the names have not been changed to protect the innocent—if anyone needed protection from my words, the words would not have been written. "Above all, do no harm" is my motto.

It is also true that I could not have published such a frank account of my mother's life while she lived; she'd have needlessly worried what her friends might think. But she no longer lives in human form, and her divine self has no worries, no fear. I know my mother would be willing for others to learn from her pain, from our pain, hence this book.

During her slow death by cancer I wrote of fear and love as honestly as I knew how. I wrote frequent letters to Harry—a real person, a true friend. In the realm of the material, Harry and I approach opposites: gender, geography, class, politics. But in the realm of the spiritual, we are more like twins: identity, growth, values, beliefs. Our friendship has grown quietly during our work together on a nonprofit board, a treasure buried within the dense forest of active lives. Our friendship flowered with the first letter, a letter written in gratitude late one night, a letter bringing such comfort to me that the ones to follow could not be helped.

After the next three letters Harry wondered what I was up to—as did I—but with his permission I continued to write, and eight months later there were forty letters in my black binder. I also sent each letter to Steve, a mentor and friend to both Harry and me, a wise presence and third soul in the process. I showed no one else—not even my husband—the letters before Mom died.

I offer these letters in the spirit in which they were written: sister to brother, friend to friend. Death touches every one of us. Perhaps what I've learned will help someone else face the inevitable transition with less fear.

When Mom informed me she was dying, I bought a new journal. The first entry reads: "And so the journey begins. Mothers and daughters and many other loving souls have traveled this road before me, and some travel now. Just take another step. Fear not."

Spring

PRIL 3, 1996

Angelkeep, Enterprise, Oregon

Dear Harry,

I heard your message on the answering machine when Keith and I returned home from Las Vegas a few hours ago, and I decided to respond in writing. While traveling through the desert with my parents in the motor home, I started a letter to you in my mind, but alas, the motivation to foster our friendship with paper and pen never materialized. Maybe now, in the silence of the midnight hour, I can share the images crowding my mind, stories from the meaningful week my husband and I spent with the dying woman who gave me birth. I know, dear friend, that you won't mind a long letter.

First of all, I want to thank you for sharing the story of your own mother's death. It is not sympathy and sentiment that sustains me, but the empathy of friends who have traveled this road already, friends who can honestly share the significance and sorrow of an intimate parting. Steve is also such a friend, as you know.

Now for a tale or two from my own incredible journey. I don't know if all dying women are lucky in Las Vegas, but my mother certainly was. Gambling is her final addiction, the one obsession—nickel and quarter bets—that she enjoys above all others. I can still hear the ringing and plunking of slot machines echoing just beyond reach, memory remnants of an intense twelve hours spent each day in casinos. She wanted above all to feel normal, to enjoy the excesses of life, to throw away time and money by pulling the lever of a mechanical box over and over, hoping for a certain sequence of programmed events: a once-in-a-lifetime chance to win ten thousand quarters. The hope gave her strength, and I followed her around like a puppy, smiling and saying yes to whatever she wanted. It was a privilege to give so freely.

"I'm your puppy," I would tell her whenever she asked how I felt, and it was true, Harry, that being with her was all I wanted. My father found some much-needed rest, fixing things and talking over the impossible odds of her survival with Keith in the motor home.

Mom's fingers turned black with dirt from the coins, and I learned to be her assistant: tearing the paper from rolls, chasing nickels that fell and hid in the red-and-blue carpet at CircusCircus, carrying the plastic tub from machine to machine. I wondered if anyone could guess that this dedicated player was dying of cancer. She was my healthy mother once again, although I watched her every move for signs of pain or fatigue.

My father said Keith and I were a godsend. He needed to move the motor home from a lot in Florence, Arizona, to their home in The Dalles, Oregon—my childhood home—and Mom needed companionship during the long drive through barren desert. Keith and I flew from Boise to Phoenix, and then we all drove nonstop to Las Vegas in the motor home. It seemed to me as if four human lives had suddenly lined up like images on the screen of a slot machine after a pull on the handle.

I understand why people gamble: The sound of bells ringing and the delightful drop of metal on metal into a steel basin—plunk! plunk! plunk!; the flash of lights and sirens that say, Yes! A winner! It really is fun to win. And so I sat with my mother and watched wild cherries spinning away, and I prayed for a little luck.

When we walked around Las Vegas, I was profoundly impressed by how many loved ones in wheelchairs were being pushed through the crowded streets. I imagined others more sick than Mom also gathered for the last hurrah—a last vacation pilgrimage to the land of dreams. Death is such a traumatic aspect of family life, and yet all families go through it, gathering and sharing memories, simultaneously saying good-bye and holding on with equal desperation. I thought of your story often, and Steve's advice that the only road lay straight ahead. "Just face it head-on," he said the night before we left to meet my folks in Phoenix. Those of us gathered in Vegas with our dying loved ones had no other choice; no amount of gambling can change the inevitable.

The drive through the desert reminded me of childhood—

a microcosm of the many years my mother and I spent talking and drinking coffee at the kitchen table, our hands busy shuffling cards. We played pinochle in the motor home while my father drove endless miles across brush and hills, and we decided those few details of departure that are possible to plan in advance: My sister can choose the ring she likes best, and I can have the picture of my mother when she was three years old.

I gently asked what kind of care she wants for the health disasters that are sure to come, but she wouldn't—she couldn't—answer. "Some decisions can only be made in the moment," she said, proving wiser than I. She has traveled this mysterious road to death with other friends and family members, so she knows how much she doesn't know.

And this makes her angry. Really angry. I had to leave the motor home on the last day to pray for strength after Mom flew into a rage. She seemed to be angry because she was dying and we were not, but I'm sure she just felt helpless. While Keith and I walked through the RV park, he wondered aloud how to approach death spiritually, and I realized the goal was to shift to a cosmic perspective, to open the mind to a broader view—an eternal and infinite view—which I did. I felt better immediately and realized this shift beyond the small universe of my human life would be an invaluable tool for the difficult weeks and months ahead. And I realized my well-grounded husband would provide a stable foundation upon which I could depend when my own emotional balance faltered.

I returned to the motor home fifteen minutes later, fortified, and determined to help my mother with her anger as well as her pain. While dealing a new pinochle hand, we apologized for being human and shared our fear about the challenges of a slow death. I was filled with gratitude for the normal sound of shuffling cards. We played and talked all afternoon while the motor home purred and rumbled across the desert. After gambling three days straight in Las Vegas, Mom left with an extra ninety dollars in her little blue purse, and I left with memories to last an eternity.

It's now three in the morning—the time limit I set for myself and this letter. During one crazy day in Las Vegas I was sure you were praying for me. I thought at the time that if mind is a spiritual system, then perhaps it would be possible to share consciousness with a friend across the miles, and I started this letter of gratitude in my head. When I returned home to find your message, this theory was confirmed.

I also thought of our friend Steve and his advice to face death head-on. I'll send a copy of this letter to him as well. I hope I've traveled a step beyond fear, but of course, I wouldn't bet on it.

Love to you both,

Janet

APRIL 9, 1996

Angelkeep

Dear Harry,

Amid the offers of Visa cards and unsolicited medical journals, I found your letter in the afternoon mail. Indeed, my friend, there are many differences between our mothers, but two things held in common stand out: the difficult challenge of facing a slow but sure death, and the almost desperate need to entertain friends until the end. Death is the great equalizer, it is true. But so is a spiritual life, which you and I hold in common despite our diverse legacies, a gift for which I am exceedingly grateful.

I thought you might be willing to read of my recent sojourn home—a time filled, once again, with vivid images and deep meanings. Memories of my mother are fully possessed when I write them down, memories that will spring to life upon the reading. And so I write without hesitation while trying to swim through a churning sea, recording the crash and strange comfort of emotional waves as the storm of death descends upon us, documenting my mother's image for those lonely days when memories are all we have. I imagine these stories describe a common experience all families share: the journey home to help a dying mother, a road most children will someday travel.

As soon as I walked in the door, she began showing me her beautiful things, suggesting what I might like, what had already been promised, and where the most unusual items came from. "The benefit of knowing," she said when I resisted claiming her treasures for my own. The benefit of dying I thought, since she won't be here to witness her children dividing her things into yours and mine, a lifetime of things that will prove a poor substitute for the wonderful woman who loved them. We spent the morning rehanging pictures, trying to match frames with spaces, shifting them to the left and then to the right.

"Give this one to my sister," she said as she slipped the wire loop through a nail on the wall. I hope I can remember.

For the first time in my life I was not a child at home. Instead of waiting for instructions, I did what needed to be done, making domestic decisions and meal plans with ease. The balance of power in my childhood home has shifted from my parents to me without resistance, it seems. We accepted our new roles with as much grace as can be found in such trying circumstances—with grateful acknowledgments instead of the usual criticisms. I reminded my mother of the cooking she did in my home after the birth of each of my three children.

"I'm spending my points," she joked, and looked at me with loving eyes.

"You taught me how to do this," I replied, desperate to give credit where credit was due.

We cooked together for three days beginning Good Friday and ending Easter Sunday. Between the creation of cookies and cupcakes, macaroni and chicken, we talked of the next life, imagining the resurrection of her own soul and the new body she would inhabit.

"Food will be perfect in heaven, Mom. You won't need an elimination system," I said while frying meatballs in olive oil. "Oh," she said, unimpressed with the biology of the afterlife. She was more worried about forgetting all she had learned in this life.

"I can't remember already," she said.

"That's a job for your soul," I assured her. My view of the soul made sense to Mom. She needed to believe that her goodness and beauty were not slipping away with her health. I promised her that nothing of value will ever be lost, and perhaps I needed reminding myself.

This was Rachel's trip; most likely my daughter's last solo pilgrimage to Grandmother's house, a truth she held quietly within the deep recesses of her young mind. She whispered questions about wigs and baldness, progressive questions I repeated aloud so she would know it was acceptable to mention disease and death around the sick and dying.

My mother talked on the phone to her friends and siblings without hesitation, saying "I'm terminal" with gentle strength. But my daughter's questions were hard for her, so I provided the answers. I explained about strong medicine and even stronger disease, about bodies that wear out and souls that wake up on the next world. My mother would have used similar terms, I'm sure, but she was unsettled by the confusion and wonder in my six-year-old's voice, and later told me—with tears in her eyes—that she worries for the grandchildren. Leaving the young to fend for themselves in a harsh world is harder than leaving the world itself, she said. But like you said, Harry, she doesn't know how hard the leaving can be. For a brief and beautiful afternoon three generations were busy talking and cooking in the kitchen, trying to face death head-on.

We froze most of the food. When Mom thought about how to spend her remaining months, she realized that having friends for dinner was her greatest pleasure, and she invited all her snowbird friends to visit. Soon, she told them; come soon. And so we prepared packages of easy-to-heat dinners, stacking bulging freezer bags on the kitchen table. We looked like a home-based catering business. Mom joked that if any food was left after her death, we could serve it at her memorial service.

"You're the only woman I know who would cook for her own wake," I teased, and then thought of hiding one package of meatballs deep in the freezer just to make it so.

My father and I had the same conversation every time we took a break. He talked about what the doctors should have done, about the mistakes and greed of the medical profession. He talked about what to do next, about a living will and his promise to help

Mom die at home. He talked about miracle cures, and then he cried because he had failed to find her a nice lily for Easter.

"There's no time left for procrastination or regrets," I said, and held my father a long while.

Slowly, I looked around at the things my mother has collected through the years; reluctantly, I wondered which of them I would like to have. And I realized I have little interest in what she finds beautiful—in the art of aesthetic sensibilities we are much different. But there are a few things that would fit well in my home. Just a few. And someday, if I have the same benefit of knowing, I'll tell my daughter whence my treasures came and imagine them upon her shelves.

I'm not sure when I will return to The Dalles. My mother's friends are sending cards and should arrive to visit any day. She hungers for the mail and the potential connection each card promises. But she is not really satisfied by the sight of words on paper—she needs the feel of arms around her. I hope her friends come soon, and I hope they run out of food.

Thanks for treasuring our friendship, Harry, something else we hold in common. Your letter was beautiful, and affirming.

Much love to you as well,

Janet

PRIL 11, 1996

Angelkeep

Dear Harry,

The stamp is hardly dry on the letter I posted this morning, but here I am again, purging heart and mind using keyboard and screen, finding my way through this challenging time. My other writing projects are now on hold. It seems I have no choice but to give myself fully to this rising obsession of writing you letters. I move and breathe in swirling stories of life with a dying woman, and rest between the telling.

My mother has no plans this weekend, since her friends have not yet returned from their southern travels. From where I stand, every minute she spends alone is wasted time. Tomorrow I drive 250 miles to see her again. Perhaps in a year I'll look back and think how foolish I was to have hurried so to meet the end; perhaps in three weeks I'll give generous thanks for the time I've had to spend with her.

Death is such a mystery. Like detectives we watch for signs of Mom's failing health and search for clues to explain her profound itching. Could it be an allergic reaction to the medication she takes? Or perhaps the cancer—inflammatory breast cancer—is spreading from chest to calves at lightning speed. Or perhaps her liver is failing, and unfiltered toxins are driving her crazy. She just wants the itching to stop. No more chemo, no more medicines, no more chances.

I never knew what "calling mother every day" was all about. I used to think the poor souls who wrote Dear Abby about parental problems just needed a life of their own. Now I know better. Fear of losing Mother drives me to the phone as soon as the rates go down each evening, and sometimes before. I remember the story about how restless you were after your own mother died, how you felt an itch to do something but didn't know what until Steve mentioned the daily phone calls you no longer made. I know someday it will be my turn to itch, to reach for the phone out of habit, to wonder what she was thinking and what she was doing and what plans she had for summer, to itch for her calm voice and good advice.

At times, Harry, our falling spirits are of more concern than her failing health. My sister called last night from a hospital in California. Her husband developed a deep infection following shoulder surgery, and his immediate future is now filled with antibiotics and rehabilitation. My mother veiled the truth of her own illness in general terms, wanting to spare her youngest daughter yet another worry. But my husband is trained as a physician and answers health questions straight on: "Weeks to months," he told Judy when she asked how long Mom had, and Judy burst into tears.

"What did you think?" I asked her when the phone was passed.

"I knew Mom wasn't going to get better when she stopped the chemo, but death in weeks to months? Why didn't someone tell me?" My sister's heart-wrenching cries soon left her breathless.

"You need a plan, Judy," I said gently. "First bring your husband home from the hospital, and then arrange for a visit." You can let a few weeks pass, I assured her, but not months.

Judy is the sentimental one in the family, and death is her enemy. Her best friend, Karen, was murdered in high school, a senseless loss at a tender age. And with the passing of each elderly relative she grieves again for her friend. "Death takes them all unfairly," she says, and gives her soul to grief, wrapping herself in things of the beloved departed and resting her mind in memories of times and places.

A few months ago we were remembering our deceased grandmother's green decor, her obsession with a certain brand of white cotton underwear, and our trips together to town on the bus. Judy talked as if she alone has these memories, as if possession were hers by right of need. But we remember different things, and the same things differently.

My mother has repeatedly asked that I accept my share of her collected treasures regardless of my seeming lack of a sentimental nature. "For your own children," she said, "it must be fair." Which is why she tries to interest me in pictures and rings when all I want is time and love.

My big brother, Don, is true to his gender and holds most of his feelings inside. I have taken to asking direct questions about his life and his fears, using the language of counselors to open doors that would otherwise remain closed. It is not my skill, however, that leads to meaningful conversation these days but a powerful need to weave strong bonds from our mutual suffering.

He and I are somewhat similar in looks and in living. Melody is to him what language is to me, and we pour ourselves into our respective arts: He sings like an angel, and I write each night in my journal. Friends and family have long said to both Don and me, "You could have done so much with your talent." Is it too late? He wonders, but not I—not in the midst of this rising obsession. Maybe he'll write a song for her.

And I'll write these letters, Harry, with a need so pressing, I can only assume the beauty of suffering is being shared as a gift, an interactive journey with my divine friends—the seen and the unseen alike.

With gratitude and love,
Janet

APRIL 15, 1996

Angelkeep

Dear Harry,

I know you have just received two letters from last week. Please don't feel obligated to respond to each one—an impossibility, given my prolific tendencies these days. I enjoy writing the letters, and if you enjoy reading them, we have a fair exchange. Just so you know, Harry, that I appreciate being able to depend on our friendship this way.

Last weekend my twelve-year-old son, Michael, traveled with me to see Mom. The drive through the Oregon countryside was beautiful: The unsettled weather of spring, with diverse and dramatic cloud formations, provided great contrast throughout the four-hour trip from the Wallowa Mountains to the Columbia River. We drove through snow, hail, rain, wind, dust, and an occasional burst of sun that highlighted distant vistas like a doorway to heaven. The Columbia River gorge was exceptional in its wildness: My son and I were captivated by swirling mists that would suddenly clear to reveal towering hills above a dancing river covered with whitecaps. For twenty years I have traveled this scenic highway to reach my childhood home and still, each time, I am awed by the beauty. The highway—which snakes more than one hundred miles along the steep banks of the mighty Columbia—was designed for beauty.

Recent flooding was still evident in some places. I was saddened to see that the lovely Riverfront Park my children enjoyed last summer was now a disaster, with benches sitting in high water and driftwood scattered across the lawn like bleached bones on a killing field. I wondered if the park was too much of a mess to clean up and had been surrendered to the elements.

Michael has a special bond with his grandmother, formed the day of his birth and strengthened throughout the dozen years they have been friends. Because of financial limitations he was born in a house across town, a birth home designed for healthy young mothers without money. I was a single mother, so I asked my mother to accompany me, and after twenty-four hours of difficult labor, I nursed my son for the first time while Mom snored on the bed next to me. The staff at the birth home encouraged us to vacate the room quickly, and within two hours of my delivery, I was waiting for a fish sandwich at the drive-through window of the nearby McDonald's and watching my newborn son sleep in the backseat of his grandmother's Lincoln, an image that never fades. That night Mother curled up with Michael to take the first watch, but sunlight was streaming through the window of my small apartment before any of us woke; the child had slept twelve hours without food in his grandmother's arms. And so it began, the sharing of a son, perhaps my mother's way to give to a male child what her own son no longer needed. I wonder if those days are ahead for me.

I made this trip so Michael and Mom would have time together. When we arrived, however, I realized my father was actually more in need than my mother, and was glad to have made the trip for him. Dad seemed older than his sixty-nine years— stooped and cheerless when we walked in the door, serving an artichoke and butter to his wife of forty-four years. I took over the domestic tasks, joking about how the maid had finally arrived. He smiled, and after my son and his grandmother were settled in matching chairs facing the television, I followed my father downstairs, intent on simply listening.

He told stories like never before: how his own father had died at age forty-four of cancer, suffering at home in the middle of a silent family, dying before my sixteen-year-old father could reach the hospital room; how his mother had willingly signed an early navy application because her son found more than his share of trouble in town; how he returned after the Second World War without a high school diploma and aced his college entry exams; how he wrecked his brother-in-law's beloved car during the very first term of his freshman year. I was surprised how like my brother he sounded—joking about his troubled past—and relieved that he was finally letting go of expectations after all these years. He remembered himself just as he was, and in the remembering became more like us—the equally flawed children who love him.

My father's cheerful voice roused me the next morning. While dressing I remembered that as children we judged the day to come by his willingness to tease and joke. By nightfall he was usually spent; a hundred irritations, both real and imagined, would take their toll. Silence in the morning was devastating. I assumed that debts from the day before had been left unpaid and were gathering interest; escape was first on my mind when I woke to silence. But irritations no longer accumulate—they rise and fall like a beating heart.

Two of my mother's five siblings, a sister and a brother, arrived with a husband and son to spend the day. While they talked with Mom, I cooked dinner and served iced tea, occasionally joining the conversation from the doorway, marveling at the flood of memories we held in common before life swept us apart, before love and fear carved a unique dimension into each of our lives. I peeled potatoes and remembered and then rushed to my room to scribble a note in my journal. If not for the fact that I have always done this, I would have felt like a spy.

Progress looks different when worn by such diverse souls. My middle-aged cousin, without a job or family, has discovered God at the church down the street; my balding uncle, still single after a difficult divorce years ago, raved about the accomplishments of his six grown children; my vivacious aunt, recovering from hip surgery, told jokes only seniors would love and hobbled around the house intent on helping me. These family members have been through everything under the sun together and, at times, have been judged too harshly for their mistakes. But they have survived, and each has a faith in God that is beautiful in its simplicity. It was a pleasure to serve them, and we laughed around the dinner table at jokes that flowed so well, I'd be a shoo-in for the grand prize on the Comedy Show if I could only remember them all. It was a dynamic family interaction, a testimony to living faith that eased the pain of death and dying for the eight of us gathered around the table.

Mom says she is more afraid of chemo than death, and jokes about having to call her friends and apologize for living if she happens to live too long. She makes a lot of jokes, and so do those who know her well. When Mom told Pastor Jim that funerals are barbaric, he quipped: "But that's how I make money for tennis shoes!"

And her friend Bob, who is also dying of cancer, said, "My wife is praying for you, Marian. That's not my cup of tea as you know, but I am thinking real hard."

Bob's comment led to a discussion of the difference between faith and religion. "Just because a person refuses to use the language of religion doesn't mean he has no faith," I said. "And besides, religions don't survive life in the flesh." And we agreed that from a spiritual perspective we are all children of God regardless of how we define our religious life. Religion has been a wedge between Mom and her siblings for years, and so the promised end to their self-imposed silence on the subject seems a blessing to her.

She also wondered aloud if criminals would survive death. I said that in my opinion, anyone who seeks God will have the chance to find him, that even a long life of crime is forgiven with the asking.

"Of course, those who neglect their spiritual life until the very end will have a lot of catching up to do in the next world—remedial training," I said, and smiled.

A shadow fell across her face, and I waited for her to speak. "We don't remember everything, do we?" she asked quietly, and I knew the reason for her question.

"We only remember that which has survival value, Mom," I said. "The pain and suffering of mortal life fades away." Another blessing she waits for.

Those who know what she's been through understand her decision not to take chemo this time. My mother has been sick most of her life: first from the trauma of witnessing her own mother's death as a seven-year-old child, then from the emotional and physical effects of anger, then from cancer possibly caused by anger—cancer that refused to be cured by surgery, chemo, and radiation, cancer that returned within a month to ravage her again. Death is her last earthly chapter, the final resolution before her promised resurrection, a time when the child she still is will greet the mother she once lost.

And even though she seems to have surrendered, to be traveling without resistance toward the end, each step is measured in meaning, with memories and treasures for all who journey with her. Many would find it hard to juggle faith and hope while straddling two worlds, including my mother, who holds to her faith and saves her hope for the next world. All we can do is understand that what she does is not surrender.

My son seems to understand. He said very little on the way home, but smiled and nodded when I tried to explain: "The suffering will be difficult, Michael, but the result will be beautiful for her." He wears a new jacket, a professional team jacket Mom bought for him as an early thirteenth birthday present. She opened her little blue purse—the one she used in Vegas—and gave me all the money inside: four crisp twenties and a ten.

"For Michael," she said. "Buy him something really nice."

He has never received a more beautiful gift except, perhaps, the gift of loving arms during his first night of life on this world. The sun was shining all the way home, and it was warm in the truck, but he left his jacket on. He was still wrapped up in Grandmother's gift long after the sweat rolled down his brow.

With all the traveling to see my mother, I've been toying with the idea of staying home this weekend instead of attending our quarterly meeting in Chicago. But the right decision is for me to live fully in the midst of Mom's dying. I know my children will do fine without me, and Keith truly enjoys his turn as the home parent. My final rationale is that I need time for myself, to be with colleagues and talk of things beyond death, and to eat something I haven't cooked myself for a change. See you there, my friend.

Love,

Janet

APRIL 23, 1996

Angelkeep

Dear Harry,

The sound of heavy rain falling on our blue metal roof surrounds the cabin with a beautiful song of comfort and refuge. I stoke up the woodstove and gaze across the fields, watching birds dance on the lawn and feast upon the bounties of spring. Does the worm know his search for life will lead to death, that his end is inevitable? Not unless the hand or beak that descends upon him does so slowly. Then he knows to fight with every fiber of his being, to survive if he can. The struggle for life exists throughout the forest: coyotes and cougars, bats and badgers, seek their own renewal through the death of another, using instinct to kill and live or die fighting.

There is no escape from the laws of biology. The cancer killing my mother is composed of living cells that feast upon others too weak to resist, relentless cells that changed form after the first chemo and continued feeding upon her flesh. They simply seek life, and my mother's death will be the grim result. The doctors say the cancer will eventually leave a rotting breast, like a carcass in the woods, and the stench will drive her crazy. How can such a small part lead to the death of the whole? we wonder while we vilify the amazing cells and bugs that kill us. We fight with chemicals— spraying fields, injecting veins, taking pills to end the siege. Sometimes it works and the noxious part is purged. Or is it?

Perhaps the world is simply one large biological organism— humans included—and the death of the parts will someday lead to a dying whole; perhaps the fight with chemical weapons creates an illusive disharmony instead of a healthy destruction; perhaps modern disease is caused by the introduction of too many killing machines, however small, that eventually attack the entire system. One by one, the chemicals we use prove poisonous to the organic body. Ignorance is no longer a viable defense, but greed still works.

Like all animals, my mother responds by striking out with anger at those who have failed to save her, an instinct to escape death by fighting the other. I suppose this letter echoes her anger and seems out of character for me. I have no fight with death,

Harry, but why must it come in such hideous form, sneaking up without warning and then leaving us to wonder when and how the end will be? My mother lives at the mercy of microscopic parts that will soon destroy her, and she feels helpless. She could fight with chemicals, but the battle would quickly kill her, and so she waits for death; she hates the wait more than she fears the death, it seems. She cries with frustration on the phone, "I'm rotting away. I'm sitting in this chair, rotting away." And then she blames the doctors who thought she was healed, and the insurance companies for not allowing enough tests, and my dad for various omissions.

My mother is two women, and I know both of them well. Sometimes I face the one who can't handle stress, who moves from slight irritation to intense anger like a quickly rising tide, filling the space between us with anguish, asking irrational questions in order to purge her heart of the pain. "Why?" she sobs, and I briefly wonder, "Why what?" But her question is rhetorical, a symbol for the secret reservoir of trauma that sits within her like oil under the ocean floor, an intense pressure occasionally released in short spurts of dark emotion.

My earliest memories are of traumatic times when she would leave for days or weeks in order to carry her anger beyond the shores of our family home. These memories occupy space in my mind—great shadows of fear and abandonment that punctuate the history of my life. But I have found a way around the shadows, and when I do look back, I see beyond my own pain to my mother's childhood, where the dead are silently buried, where the pressure began to build.

Because I understood her pain I was not injured by it, and this understanding seemed to reside in me as a natural gift. At twelve I learned to sit with Mom when the tides of anger would rise, and help her find release over endless cups of coffee and pinochle games. Without comment I would listen until she was fully spent, and then provide comfort by giving voice to a pain she could no longer resist; sharing pain became part of our life together. At times she found no reason to live and would threaten to end it all. More than once I visited her in hospital rooms, and she would scream at me: "Why are you here; you don't care!" But I did, of course, and refused to take her words personally. I saw Mom as a seven-year-old child crying for Mother, and held her as close as I could, sometimes with words alone. We were sisters from the beginning, and we traded the role of mother back and forth whenever the need arose. She lived without her own mother most of her life, and I was honored to fill those shoes for her on occasion.

As a result, my mother and I have no unfinished business; we have given each other as much as there is to give. But the days ahead frighten me, Harry. I'm afraid her dark emotion will fill the last few weeks of our life together with more pain than we can handle. An unreasoned fear, I know, but I'm trying to face my fear head-on.

Yesterday we talked on the phone for hours, trading ideas back and forth in an effort to fill the empty days. We explored and dismissed every option except one: She wants to be with friends and family while she feels well enough to sit and talk. The only meaning left in Mom's life is found in the one undeniable need we all share, a universal truth: Relationship is living; everything else is what we do in order to have relationships.

When she's alone and death descends, she feels like a frightened child watching her own mother die; in solitude the well of pain within her heart is tapped again. I don't know if more purging will relieve her or just wear her out. What I do know is that she loves without hesitation, and such love has always been enough for me, even in the midst of great pain.

It's still raining outside, solid sheets of spring rain that seem a welcome release of unshed tears. When I finish wrapping myself in the comfort of weather and memory, I'll heat a pot of soup on the stove and bake a loaf of bread. Thanks for listening, my friend.

Much love,

Janet

PRIL 26, 1996

Angelkeep

Dear Harry,

In this mountain valley spring unfolds like the early morning of a new day, infused with potential after a long and sometimes fitful sleep. The dormant landscape slowly awakens as the season evolves; sleeping animals and new babes emerge amid sporadic showers of rain and snow. The awakening seems like an encompassing dream, a memory from the mind of nature that embraces all existence in the cycle of life. There is beauty everywhere the eye wanders.

Green fields—fluorescent with new growth—roll across the valley toward the dense forest. Here and there large barns painted red with white trim stand amid a cluster of grain silos and plowing machines; young fillies, nursing calves, and little black lambs frolic about. The valley is bordered by snow-capped mountains that stand six thousand feet above family farms, an embrace of immutable rock that has provided protection and isolation to every generation willing to work the land.

The mountains look like mentors, standing firm in fresh coats of spring snow while the elements rage and play. Clouds swirl and weave around the peaks and then part for pastel beams that highlight the ragged summit from above. Surely God must have a hand in such celestial scenes, I think, and watch the dance of colors over the valley: white and blue and pink above fluorescent green and barn red.

The snow line rises midway up the mountain; the warm ground surrounding our cabin melts the occasional showers of spring snow with ease. Iris bulbs shoot heavy stems and thick leaves eight inches above rich soil, and wild roses—with red stems and lime green leaves—prove that spring is finally here. The ponds are muddy and streams flow swiftly, cresting their banks in the usual places and casting a symphony of sound that fairly rivals a raging river; our voices are captured and drowned.

Thick mud reveals the tracks of animals that have wandered down our trails. Waking with hunger and dense with sleep, those who hibernate soon remember that humans with dogs also live on the mountain. Lone cougars roam beyond their normal boundaries, motivated by hunger and increasing numbers. They are no longer hunted and have become the newest menace to those of us living on the edge of the Oregon wilderness. Black bears tear apart dead stumps looking for insects to feed their young; we discover large piles of fresh scat around the ponds and raise our voices just in case a protective mother is foraging nearby. Coyotes move in fearless packs, calling to cousins with a series of long howls and short yelps in the dead of night.

In the morning we hear squirrels that chirp like birds and birds that cry like a referee's whistle, waking us at sunrise. This particular morning brings a sense of renewal as sunshine streams through the front window, lighting the faded area on the cabin couch. I sit with coffee and the remnants of sweet dreams, wondering what I have already forgotten; I sit with small beings who wake and reach for me, beautiful children who nestle across my warm belly and whisper scenes from their own sweet dreams. With every whisper we immerse ourselves in the unfolding of a new day, in the cycle of life.

Hope all is well with you, my friend.

Much love,

Janet

APRIL 29, 1996

Angelkeep

Dear Harry,

Loss of dignity is not one of the options we willingly entertain when reviewing the evolution of a human life. It is the unspoken horror, the quiet suffering behind closed doors that we refuse to recognize in order to spare our loved ones shame. I know the choice is personal for every child of God—defined by relationships and rationale—but I would spare myself this loss if I could and plead only for the option to choose my own end, not for the deed itself.

Anyway, thanks for your letter. As you can see, the story you told of your own mother's suffering has touched me deeply, like everything else these days. An expanding circle of meaning seems to capture the normal events of my ordinary life and recast them as significant—the influence of impending death in the family. Emotion rests on the surface of my existence like oil on water, and I struggle to refine an essence worth saving. Reaching back provides enough strength to move forward; like respiration, my mind opens to embrace memory and then closes to process and purge. In the purging I write and feel blessed that the results are not tossed in a dresser drawer somewhere. Writing helps more than you know, Harry, so here I am again, with gratitude as usual.

The roads I often traveled in childhood—but rarely noticed—once brought settlers across a continent. Near the end of the journey pioneers stood on the banks of the Columbia River and wondered whether to test their fate by river or cross the Cascade Range before early snow closed the trails. Lewis and Clark were two of the first. Most decided to build rafts and many died—the rapids, now dammed and bridged, were too wild on some days for any to survive.

Wind still howls down the Columbia River gorge, causing trees to grow one-sided and whitecaps to dance on the water. It's not hard to imagine entire families on makeshift rafts piled high with chairs and dressers and wagons-in-parts, tossing about on the waves, terrified. Whitecaps seem so tame from a distance, playful and picturesque, but waves push and pull with abandon when wearing white crowns, dumping saints and sinners alike beyond redemption. The volume of water that flows to the sea through this majestic channel is the second greatest on the entire North American continent. Without a doubt, wagon axles and iron pots rest on the riverbed, awaiting salvage along with artifacts from more ancient times.

Villages—now buried by dozens of dams—have stood along the banks of this mighty river for ten thousand years, a continuous habitation unprecedented in the region. Nearby cities and cultures have come and gone, but those who love the river have always been here; we know for sure that five hundred generations have sailed and fished the Columbia, and can only wonder how many others have lived and died on her banks before them.

My parents live on a hill overlooking the river, with Mount Adams striking a dramatic pose in the center of a sweeping vista, an incredibly beautiful scene that I appreciate more with each viewing. As children, we often watched the tugboats push barges up and down the river, silent ships full of mysterious cargo. Now we also watch the windsurfers who have discovered the gorge and dominate the local economy. There are little windsurfer pictures on all the highway exits and a dozen new parks.

Saturday morning was a perfect wind day, and we watched small beings on colorful boards fly across the water like birds—bouncing on whitecaps and slicing through waves as we drove along the river. The strength and skill required for this sport seems a testimony to the human spirit, a triumph of mind and muscle over wind and waves. We also passed driftwood piled high at Riverside Park, and I was relieved to see that time and money had been found to clean the beach after the flood, another reality of the new economy.

The children and I arrived in The Dalles a few minutes before the Cherry Festival parade; we slowly traveled down main street in our white Suburban while families set up lawn chairs on the sidewalk. Vendors pushed carts loaded with toys and balloons—a great temptation for my children—but we decided to go directly to Grandma's, even though we were an hour early.

"You rescued me," she said as we walked in the door. "I was just losing my cool over HMOs. It's their fault, you know; they could have done something."

Mom was obsessing about a recent news program exposing business barons stealing health care dollars and was working her way back to livid when we arrived. The children settled her down with hugs and "Hello, Grandma!" and she began to live again. Alone and angry is the same as sick and dying for Mom, but she shifts like magic when people are near.

The challenges of dying—weakness, pain, itching, medication—are being resolved, and Mom seems to be living more fully while she waits to die. Doctors are last on her list of honorable characters, however, so when her oncologist recommended a female internist in town, Mom refused to pursue the referral. But the internist called Mom and promised to help her die at home.

"And by the way," her new doctor said, "I was a hospice nurse in Montana for twenty-five years"—just a few miles from Mom's childhood home and a short drive from where her own mother died. Keith calls this kind of coincidence "angel work," and I pretend to wonder.

Clothes have always been important to Mom. After the early death of her mother, her father cared for the six children—including an infant—alone on a dusty Montana farm. Money was scarce and their wardrobe was scavenged from a box of relief clothes in town; the concept of welfare was still a generation away. Mom often speaks of the humiliation she felt and of her sacred vow never to let her own children suffer for a lack of new clothes. True to her word, my sister and I wore matching dresses and hats to the mandatory nursing home visits with our great-aunt and great-uncle, and to church every Sunday. I hated the dresses and never really appreciated the passion with which my mother presented us; even today it takes great effort for me to dress fashionably—a lingering rebellion—and my girls wear mostly hand-me-downs from friends, much to my mother's chagrin. Ah, the circles we weave.

Nothing Mom has in her three closets can now be worn over her tender chest, except a white nylon pantsuit that Dad washes every other day while she waits in a bathrobe. "Would you shop for me?" she asked when I arrived.

Despite the parade, I traveled from store to store, through crowds and clowns and traffic jams, searching for another pantsuit. With determination I went from rack to rack and finally found two jackets in an obscure store hidden among booths and balloons—not what she asked for but far more fashionable than what she was wearing. I was elated and so was she when she saw them. Angel work, I thought.

"They're perfect, don't you think?" I asked again and again, basking in the joy of dressing a loved one well.

Mom suggested we all go to the carnival. Dad and I were surprised that she expressed interest in such a public event, but we made plans for the following day. Pain erupted with force in the morning, however, so I packed up the kids and went without her.

"Too much money and not enough fun," I grumbled amid the blowing dust and gaming displays designed to break the family bank.

"Try to enjoy yourself," said Michael, who tired of my impatience and anger.

Imagine my surprise when I turned around and found my folks smiling at me; Mother looked dashing in her new jacket and wig. She bought sno-cones and corn dogs for the children and waited happily while they rode the Hammer and the Gravitron. Harry, it's hard to describe the feeling of being together on a warm spring day, having fun once again as a family—perhaps for the last time in such form. We snapped picture after picture, storing our earthly treasures in a small metal canister, and walked arm in arm across uneven ground—across packed dirt, broken pavement, and shattered glass.

"You rescued me," I told her, and felt more like her child than ever before.

We tried to say good-bye in the parking lot, but I burst into tears without warning and found Michael crying with unusual abandon when I climbed into the driver's side of the Suburban.

"Leaving is harder this time, isn't it?" I said, and lost my composure again. "We're too emotional to travel just yet," I yelled to Mom out the car window, and she told us to come to the house, which we did. Dad comforted me in the kitchen, talking about the inevitability of death, while Michael and Mom made plans for the future: He'll travel alone on the train to see her.

And so goes the trading of roles with my mother. Back and forth we give what we can and find release in the arms of the other.

It was good to feel like a child again, despite the tears. Talk to you soon, Harry, and thanks so much for the book.

With love and gratitude as always,

Janet

AY 2, 1996

Angelkeep

Dear Harry,

It's snowing outside, believe it or not, so I've started a fire in the woodstove to warm myself. Yesterday—May Day—was filled with sunshine and stress, but today it's mostly snow and solitude. I sit alone with a blank screen and wonder how I'm feeling; without some immediate problem to wrestle with I seem a bit numb—except for the pain in my jaw that comes from clenching my teeth.

I have no doubt that transition is designed like a game of dominoes when I review the long line of personal problems trailing behind me. Each member of my family brings a new challenge—work, school, friends—so I've finally stopped trying to manage everything. I give myself without resistance to the experiences that fall one upon the other and let emotions flow like spring runoff; a seasonal thing, I've decided.

This morning I held my youngest daughter, Hannah, for a long while and gained primal satisfaction from rubbing her cheek against my own. In the center of my being a mysterious process transforms the soft touch of baby skin into fuel for the mother machine. My need for this fuel gives Hannah another reason for being—a way of belonging to a reality much larger than herself, a spiritual exchange impossible to replace in any material way: We all need to be needed.

Perhaps spiritual growth relates directly to how much we allow ourselves to be needed. So now I'll stop complaining and learn to juggle the demands of my loved ones better. In fact, I'll give thanks that they need me so much. Service, service, and more service—regarding this truth, Harry, you are an inspiration.

The dentist will soon call to suggest I stop clenching my teeth and to schedule an appointment to cap two broken molars—casualties of my stress war. This afternoon I'll take a walk, count blessings, and think about transition: Perhaps the only way to grow beyond limits is to push myself beyond them.

Have a great weekend. I hope you can enjoy some time cheek to cheek with your kids—or maybe they think they're too old for that now? I'm planning to read a novel.

Much love,

Janet

AY 6, 1996

Angelkeep

Dear Harry,

After we spoke today, I cultivated the wild strawberries that grow along the rock terrace behind our cabin—digging up clumps of sod, separating grass stems from strawberry plants, shaking soil loose and smoothing the surface of the new bed, poking holes with my index finger and gently laying young plants to rest. Some of the plants consisted of two leaves and a few roots—hardly enough to call a plant—but like pioneers, wild plants can survive in new soil as long as the roots are attached. I imagined myself a pioneer, with possessions discarded along the Oregon Trail, finding bounty in the wilderness: Water, wood, and wild plants provide necessities of homesteading even in the twentieth century.

As my hands worked soil warmed by the sun and still muddy from melting snow, my mind wandered through memories of childhood and images of my father: The logical man I knew as a child has blossomed into a sentimental soul able to forgive all he has endured during four decades of a mysterious marriage.

The mystery consists of diversity: two human beings as different as night and day, struggling through the currents and rapids of a shared emotional life, finding the will to keep a family together in the midst of recurring storms. Each of my parents created their own escape, and both depended on me for companionship.

After long days drinking coffee and playing cards with my mother, I sometimes spent long nights at the same table with my father, talking politics and psychology late into the evening while he drank a few beers. Besides the mental stimulation of our midnight talks, there was the potential for small encouragements and expressions of love that were left unsaid in the daylight hours.

In order to make sense of our unique relationships, I grew fond of saying my mother taught me to love and my father taught me to think, but of course, few things are this simple. Thinking and feeling cannot be divided into two distinct camps, as much as I have tried. Perhaps this division served me well in my youth by providing a limit to expectations—a way of viewing the strength of each parent without becoming distracted by their shortcomings—but I have finally come to understand that limiting my perception to expression is a mistake: Who can tell by looking how much love or logic rules? Emotions run deep beneath the smooth surface of the calm water, and the mind moves fast when faced with the rapids. I work to find peace in my own life by combining these parts—by thinking clearly when feeling intense emotions, and feeling deeply when trying to figure things out.

There was little peace between my parents during the early

years, unfortunately, but plenty of love in the family, and hence the mystery. To my young mind their lack of peace was a failure, and I always wondered what comfort my parents found in their companionship. What they loved about each other was hidden from view, but they carried a set of values in common: honesty, kindness, fairness. They made mistakes in life with each other, but these mistakes were never extended to the children; I did not wonder if my parents loved me, only how they loved each other.

My father was an electrical engineer, an expert in the transfer of power from the northern river to the southern desert, and so we lived along the Columbia River most of our lives. I never seemed to notice. The universe I lived in as a child did not include the beauty of the river or the gorge, though we often traveled this scenic highway along the border of Oregon to reach my childhood home in Portland. I cared whether my parents were getting along, when I would see my friends, whether a certain boy liked me, but I cared little for nature and would tilt my head curiously when people remarked on our beautiful view. A river and some hills, sometimes a view of the mountain ... what's the big deal? I wondered. But now I've fallen in love with nature, and with history as well. Is this simply advancing age or an awakening of some seed planted long ago?

Memories of our life on the Columbia River now crest the banks of my subconscious and seep into my mind like floodwaters, filling the empty spaces of my forgotten childhood with images of a silent and powerful love, a gift from my father. Although he rarely expressed a passion for people, he must have loved the river. When I was twelve, he bought a small boat—eighteen feet with six seats—and I have fond memories of weekend trips to sun and ski on calm water. He preferred to fish, however, and I have bittersweet memories of sunrise expeditions with coolers and poles and a churning stomach. Like a chauffeur for a time, I drove the boat at a snail's pace while he trolled the river for salmon.

Sometimes we crossed the Pacific bar in our small craft and bounced through six-foot waves that broke over the windshield while Dad bailed and laughed and hoped out loud that we would catch a big one. Alive he was with pole in hand, mixing his passion with anticipation like all who fish the river and sea. I became fearless and have since wondered at this gift of life I still possess after so much youthful folly. But those are other stories, Harry, some of which you already know.

When I was nineteen, my mother won a large jackpot in Reno and gave the money to my father, another mystery. He bought a thirty-six-foot cabin cruiser, and our summer trips across the ocean bar were never again life-threatening. He would catch the fish, gut them, and toss them below for me to fry; standing upright in rough water was hard enough without trying to maneuver a spatula and pan, but somehow I managed. Mom had a weak stomach and needed to breathe fresh air above deck, so I learned to submerge my own queasiness. Besides, like my father frequently said, I was the one with the strong stomach.

We must have traveled a thousand miles on the river between The Dalles and Astoria, the same route that pioneers traveled on makeshift rafts in the mid-1800s, the same route that locals enjoyed aboard majestic stern-wheelers during the next fifty years. River travel was the only way to reach the cities and towns that have slowly disappeared from the Columbia's banks. Commerce defines the life of a city, and so the transition from river traffic to railroad and truck left many old towns along the Columbia to legend and decay; the few thriving waterfront towns that remain have the good fortune to sit by a bridge or a dam, including The Dalles, which has both nearby. And now we harness the wind for sport, and so goes the evolution of a river economy: from pioneers to fishermen to timber barons to wheat farmers to windsurfers. The river has carried them all through the years, including my family.

My father is now too old to manage the boat by himself, a fact that saddens him greatly. My brother lives in Portland—where the old cabin cruiser is moored on the river—but he has little time left for fishing. During his teenage years, Don spent countless hours at the helm while Dad fished, but he left home at eighteen, joined the navy, married, and became a parent himself before he was twenty.

As the oldest child at home it was my turn to fish, and the seeds of my river love were sown then, I believe: sown in the thrill of rough water and the desire to please my father; nurtured by the gentle rock and roll of waves during endless hours at the helm; remembered with the harvest of a waning life, when memories flow beyond the banks designed to hold such treasures in trust. My turn has become a treasure in hindsight: I cherish every wind we wrestled to fish the river and every wave we rode to reach the sea.

Harry, the life cycle of a river is a beautiful image, a metaphor for eternity. When I finish this letter I'll fill a watering can in the mountain stream—the headwaters of a tributary that will eventually find its way to the Columbia and out to sea—and give the wild strawberries a drink. And then I'll sit on the bridge below the cabin and watch springwater dance over stones: water that flows down the mountain into creeks, across fields, through air; water that nourishes the bodies of all who reside upon this world. I'll remember my childhood on the banks of the Columbia and feel my way back home, back to the steady wind and wild waves of a beloved river, back to the source of my passion for nature.

My father has changed a lot since our days fishing the Columbia, and can finally express his love for others with ease. And he cares for my mother with such affection that I find a sense of closure for the questions of love and marriage I have carried since childhood. Now, when Mom's anger erupts without warning, he says he understands how she feels and tries to help as best he can. The arguments have ceased and the love has endured.

A good marriage must be like a mighty river, with currents and rapids and a changing commerce. My parents are nearing the final sea and will approach the bar in a vessel that has withstood a lifetime of wind and waves. I feel blessed to have sailed with the love and counsel of such worthy souls—seasoned sailors who have traveled with courage upon the waters of life.

It's a beautiful day here on the mountain, filled with sunshine and serenity. I have an hour to water strawberries before I meet the children at school. Thanks for listening, Harry.

With love,

Janet

MAY 13, 1996

Angelkeep

Dear Harry,

Mother's Day was beautiful: A brilliant blue sky entertained soft white clouds, and the air was infused with warmth. The family tackled domestic chores while I planted flowers in several hollowed-out tree trunks that sit along the streams. We now have pansies, petunias, geraniums, lobelias, and a variety of other colorful plants waiting to bloom.

My love of spring lies dormant like wild mushrooms and mountain flowers until the first warm day in May when dynamic forces—warmth, moisture, light—suddenly converge, and the world begins to vibrate with the energy of new growth. And then I feel so fully alive that the stress and trauma of human transition fades away, replaced by the sense of renewal that comes with the spring. A beautiful word, "spring": to move or leap forward, to come into being, to emerge suddenly, to arise from a source, to return after stress, a time of growth.

The day before was more difficult. In the middle of my seven-year-old's birthday party—after she had just finished opening her gift from Grandma—my mother called to say good-bye: Life was unbearable, and she was headed to a motel room with a sack of pills. "By the time you get here, I'll already be gone," she screamed before she hung up without saying good-bye. A one-minute, one-sided conversation that ruined my day and reminded me of the many times in childhood I listened to a death wish from my sometimes irrational mother. Just one more lesson in duality, I told myself, and wrestled with what to do.

At times my mother seems like a hungry child crying in church, and I am forced to choose between feeling irritated because she disturbs my peace or understanding that her hunger is beyond her control. A familiar battle rages inside my head: to hold or release blame, to behave like a child of man or a child of God. Releasing blame is a skill I cherish, but still the test challenges me. Why today, of all days? My brother called, my cousin called, my sister called, and then, after a couple of hours, I called my mother. She sounded numb and chided me for ruining her granddaughter's birthday party, an apology designed as a joke because the truth hurt too much. I laughed and the air was cleared as it always is: with the forgiveness of sisters.

The rage has lived inside my mother longer than I have known her, born the day her own mother died and developed throughout a lifetime of guilt, blame, anger, occasional rage, and more guilt; a vicious cycle that may only end with her death. Mom told me she was closer to the deed than ever before, but a surprise visit by generous neighbors stalled her plan, another example of angel work. With coat and pills in hand Mom answered a knock on the door and felt obligated to invite the old clockmaker and his wife in for a visit. The woman was a stranger, but the man had delivered handmade gifts to my folks on two occasions. Mom was honest about her intentions and comforted by their good advice: Read the Bible when you feel despair, they said. Mom's not a reader, but she loves the Bible anyway and believes it is the word of God. And I believe these two kindhearted people were sent by angels to comfort my mother in her time of need. She pretends to wonder— why today of all days?—but not I.

The challenge presented by Mom's slow and painful demise

has only begun, I believe. Her anger seems to grow with the malignancy, a childhood death issue left unresolved. I take comfort in Steve's frequent comment regarding intransigent human weakness: something to work out in the next life. But how she leaves this life is still a difficult question.

My suspicion regarding Mom's threat was confirmed in subsequent conversations: She believes suicide is a sin unless you are out of your mind. "It's the only way I'll have the courage to do it," she said. I told her I believe the exact opposite: Taking your life in the midst of anger and rage might be an evil deed, but choosing a merciful end to a long suffering is not—it is simply a self-directed transition. "An SDT," my dad said with a much-needed laugh when I told him my thinking on the subject.

Rain showers have nourished the flowers I planted yesterday. It was a strangely symbolic weekend with Mother's Day, Rachel's seventh birthday, and Mom's suicide threat all within forty-eight hours. My heart goes out to my mother. I'm beginning to pray like you did, Harry, that the end is swift—that spring comes soon to renew my mother.

Much love,

Janet

AY 16, 1996

Angelkeep

Dear Harry,

"A sense of irritation," you said, at knowing the results but not the cause of my mother's irrational behavior. Fair enough, but fairness has actually held me from telling the full story of my mother's emotional storms; she is two women, as I have said before, and both are impressive in opposite ways. The intensity of her rage coexists with her profound love of others: One cannot be viewed fairly without the other. Our relationship is formed of both pain and love, woven together in such a way that the resulting strength is immeasurable, a wonder unless you know the whole story.

In the depths of pain I discovered myself, and in the heights of love I discovered her. This may be hard to understand with words alone, but picture the depths and heights and imagine our relationship spanning the entire spectrum, like a pendulum swinging—the more suffering we shared the more love we found. Strange but true for most relationships, unless the hand of blame grabs hold. And then—oh, dark night!—time stops and relationships sit in limbo, sometimes challenged by the push and pull of anger and recriminations, but never gaining momentum. I fear the dark and the stagnation, so I embrace the pain to reach the light and release the blame to feel my life moving somewhere.

My mother offered unconditional love, the most valuable gift, because she understood the need for love and forgiveness more than most. The irrational blame she carried for her mother's death rose without warning and surrounded her loved ones on occasion. Forgiveness was my shield: I learned early that when I held forgiveness in my heart, her anger could not penetrate my sense of self. And she would always return to her usual place as my loving mother as if nothing had happened, and that would make it easier for me. What child would think to blame the sun for a tornado? Like weather, forces beyond control would rise and fall without warning, and we learned to survive the storms. Counselors might cry, Denial! and they would be right. I have denied blame, fought it with all of my being because it terrorized my mother so much. Here is the story:

When she was seven and living on that dusty Montana farm with her parents and five siblings, both she and her mother came down with pneumonia. They were poor country farmers and were sent to the county hospital, a sterile and barren place made tolerable for a frightened child by the fact that her mother lay close at hand.

"Don't worry, Marian," she surely said to her daughter that first night. "Everything will be all right." I imagine my little Rachel, with blond curls and missing teeth, lying in a hospital bed, and my heart goes out to the child Mom was sixty-one years ago, the child who was sick and frightened and depending on her own sick mother in the next bed for her only comfort.

My mother improved over the course of a week, but her mother succumbed to the illness and slowly deteriorated. Medicine was practiced without antibiotics in 1933, so a serious infection meant certain death. As the fever raged, the grandmother I never knew became delirious, shouting and cursing at her terrified daughter and crying in pain. They finally wheeled the child from the room amid the frantic cries of her irrational mother: "Don't leave me, Marian! Please, don't leave me!" I imagine my tiny mother pleading to remain, reaching with both arms toward her dying mother as the door closed between them. She never saw her mother again.

The trauma of traveling the road to death and then surviving while her beloved mother died was too much for this seven-year-old child. Imagine the homecoming back at the farm: six motherless children under the age of eight, left to fend for themselves while a grieving father buried his young wife. The family stayed on the farm another year and then moved to a city nearby. During the next two years Mom lived the life of a poor city child with relief clothes and food boxes; guilt surely rose within her as a defense against grief. If only her mother had not died! If only she had saved her! In the dark recess of her troubled heart she blamed herself; she blamed her mother.

The family moved to Oregon when Mom was eleven, and

she started the fifth grade at Capitol Hill Elementary. Her paternal grandmother built a restaurant called the Steerhead, where the entire family eventually worked. Her father is remembered by all as a kindhearted man, and I have vague memories that this was so; he died of heart failure when I was nine.

Mom left home when her dad remarried—she was seventeen years old and had a job with an oil company, where she made friendships that have lasted a lifetime. When she was twenty-seven she married my father and gave birth to my brother a few months later. Dad's mother was a no-nonsense immigrant from Europe who felt he married beneath himself—trapped by poor judgment. I sincerely loved my only grandmother and share this family secret in order to explain how difficult the marriage was from the start—Dad's mother blamed my mother for ruining his life. More blame.

My mother's emotional storms started soon after. They form my earliest memories and my most vivid dreams: arguments, hysterics, flight, abandonment. My childhood is recorded from scene to scene, dozens of them, where tension would build and explode and then life would return to normal for a while. It is the normal I have trouble remembering, however. The experiences wrapped in the most emotion have lodged themselves in memory most firmly, while the daily kindnesses of loving parents have been absorbed into the essence of my being without fanfare. For this, I am grateful. To forget and then forgive is much harder to do than to forgive and then forget, as my mother's experience has shown me. She remembers little about her mother or life before her mother's death, and because she forgets who she was, she cannot forgive who she is. She never talks of her mother with her siblings, all of whom are still living; she refuses, in fact. "Why talk of someone I don't remember," she says with a familiar set of jaw. We know not to push her where she feels pained to go.

The other side of my mother is love personified. I remember a story wrapped in emotion of a different color, a story of selfless love that serves as a microcosm of her mothering. We were sunbathing at Rooster Rock Park on the Columbia River when I was ten, a scorching hot day that was perfect for river play. Dad was working out of town—which he often did during the early years—and Mom promised to take the three of us to the drive-in movies, an entire day and night of fun. Near midafternoon, however, Mom became violently ill with sun poisoning, an affliction similar to a serious stomach flu, and lay on the beach completely incapacitated by fever, headache, and dry heaves. What should we do? Don was only thirteen, too young to drive.

"Do you know how?" my mother asked him.

"Yes," he said sheepishly. So my brother drove us home, twenty slow miles on the interstate freeway with a sick mother bundled in the backseat. I was frightened beyond words.

When we finally reached home, safe and sound, the disappointment set in—we would miss the drive-in movie. Mom offered a deal: "You children clean up and get everything ready for the movie—snacks, blankets and pillows, pajamas for little sister. I'll rest a while and then we'll go."

You would need to know how sick she was to realize what a sacrifice she made and the much-needed trust she established as well. And herein lies the significance: My mother, who left us alone on many occasions because of emotional trauma beyond her control, put her physical needs aside in order to meet our emotional needs; she proved to us that she would put her children first whenever she could. And this has always been true.

Mom was such a loving person that my friends would often visit her. They preferred to sit and talk with Mom than come downstairs and hang with me, which was fine because I was usually reading a novel. She was humbled by intense emotion and, as a result, would treat struggling adolescents like real people. Between snacks and stories, she would empathize with the pain of their transition and offer love and advice just like a big sister.

But her personal life became public knowledge in high school. To head off emotional storms, Mom would imagine physical ailments and try to find a medical cause. She was hospitalized more times than I can count and had unnecessary surgery as a result. "Is Marian in the hospital again?" my friends often asked. I would nod and rush home to wash laundry and cook meals. These were difficult times, but I don't remember them with anxiety or anger. I did for her what she did for me; an even exchange, it seemed.

After repeated tests she was finally diagnosed with hypoglycemia, a blood-sugar disorder that causes mood swings, but the diagnosis did little to relieve her pain. There may have been a combination of causes, including chemical imbalances easily treated, but she wanted to blame a physical disease, not an imbalance. As a result, her common problems were left to rage while uncommon solutions were pursued to no avail. And now, as we know, she has her chance; disease has lodged itself upon her breast and spread to her delicate lungs. She'll most likely die of the same ailment that claimed her mother: pneumonia. She blames the doctors who failed to save her, and perhaps there were mistakes—the evolution of her cancer seems, in hindsight, a tragedy of errors.

Two years ago Mom found a lump in her breast. Mammography did not reveal what she could feel, and weeks went by before ultrasound and a biopsy confirmed the diagnosis: breast cancer. And so began a rigorous battle. The surgeon performed a lumpectomy instead of a mastectomy, even though my parents repeatedly asked that he do what appeared necessary in the operating room. When he finished the surgery, he told my father she would most likely need a mastectomy later; my parents were furious that he didn't take the breast then. But after radiation and chemotherapy, baldness and blisters, nausea and exhaustion, she was pronounced in remission.

Over the next few months her hair grew as well as her spirits, but she was troubled by a rash that was developing over the surgery site. Nerves, said one doctor; depression, said another; infection, said a third. They went from doctor to doctor, trying to heal the rash with ointments and antibiotics. Finally, a dermatologist did a biopsy and discovered inflammatory breast cancer, the fastest-growing cancer there is.

They rushed her to the hospital the same day and immediately gave her more chemo, a lot more chemo. Her hair fell out for the second time, and she suffered at least ten additional side effects. When she called me from the hospital room, she said her mouth was so dry and filled with blisters, she could hardly swallow; her skin itched and she was scratching herself raw; she was overcome by nausea, diarrhea, and vomiting. When she called again from the hospital room she sounded overwhelmingly depressed.

The doctors immediately searched for more cancer and found it. During the six months they were trying to find a diagnosis for the rash on her breast, the cancer had spread to her lungs as well. "No more!" Mom said when she heard the news, and she returned to her home in The Dalles to die.

Harry, I've heard this story a dozen times in various forms from both my parents over the past three months. I've seen the bills, read the charts, envisioned the face of each doctor examining Mom's deadly breast and finding nothing. It is impossible for me to blame them; medicine is an imperfect science, and the doctors have families just like mine. But I understand how she feels—how she has felt for a lifetime—and only wish she could find some peace before the end.

The blame she carries from childhood has crippled her to some degree, and yet in the midst of adversity she has found the strength to love others without hesitation. When I wonder how to describe our relationship without painting pictures of blind loyalty to a mother's dysfunction, I have visions of dynamite and a tunnel through rock—the channel we forged through pain with love brought light to both our lives. I have opened my mind to the strength found in suffering, and she has opened her heart to the power of love; her healing awaits the next life, and my understanding expands even now. She has taught me to love—to suffer and love—and for this I will always be grateful.

I hope this letter helps diminish your sense of irritation—a hunger for understanding, I believe. The fine line between meddling and mentoring is difficult to walk, my friend, but you do it well. Many thanks.

With loving regards,

Janet

Dear Harry,

Last weekend we met my parents in La Grande—partway between The Dalles and Enterprise—to spend a rainy day. Mom and I played pinochle all afternoon in our motel room while the girls practiced life with a family of toys and went for walks with Grandpa. Keith and Michael arrived in the evening for dinner; we ate enchiladas at a local restaurant and talked of our various travels across the Mexican border. It seemed quite strange to be acting so normal. Human beings possess a spectacular ability to adapt to any situation, to rise above traumatic experience and re-create the familiar. I imagine some prison guards are greatly challenged by the instinct to develop friendships with the incarcerated; the human spirit can transcend the most difficult hardships in order to share love with the other—a spiritual status quo.

As usual, the trauma of the week before was left behind, but I have to say, Harry, that something was lost this time; intimacy, perhaps. Mom's most recent emotional outburst was not designed to purge and reconnect but to disconnect, and she found some success. A part of her is gone already, but this is how a slow dying unfolds: In bits and pieces our strength and joy and presence of mind diminish, leaving a shadow of self that eventually gathers the remaining crumbs of human existence and flees the material form, sometimes after one or two last words. I wonder how many human beings have whispered the word "love" with their last breath: I love you; love each other. I wonder how many of us would, if we could. A beautiful way to envision our final moments of life in this form, don't you agree?

We woke to unrelenting rain on Sunday. I hesitate to complain about the rain, knowing how parched and fire-prone the southern states are, but we are drowning here, trying to absorb twice the annual rainfall in the first six months of the year. Although there have been no additional floods, roads are sliding, gardens are rotting, and we are dragging ourselves from bed every morning to the depressing sound of rain on the roof. Steve thinks it may be the apocalypse complete with drought and floods, but I think it's just a cleansing of sins; I'm planning to build an ark.

One advantage of soggy ground is the opportunity to see the tracks of animals so clearly—I'll find the pairs for my ark with ease. Keith and I followed the prints of two elk yesterday; their hoofs molded mud two inches deep as they traveled the game trail together. We also found the tracks of deer and coyote, and the faint lines of ground dwellers running across the trail from hole to stump. We discovered scat from a variety of mountain dwellers:

Coyotes drop piles of dark clay, black bears leave large mounds of green mush, and the deer and elk deposit two distinct sizes of brown beads in the middle of the trail. A delightful wilderness pastime, scat hunting.

Keith is clearing a trail he named for me—Janet's Trail— that snakes around four old-growth trees on the property, trees that were rooted on this land before any of my kind had ever seen the valley or the surrounding mountains. We estimate the age of the grandmother trees to be two hundred years or older. They were growing on this piece of land we now call home before Captain Gray sailed his boat, *The Columbia,* across the bar at the mouth of the river in 1792. He was the first American to enter the river, which is ten miles wide at the mouth. Explorers from Spain, Russia, and England traveled the Pacific coastline and spied the wild water, but none were willing to enter before Gray crossed the bar on the morning of May 11, and thus laid claim to river and land for the United States of America.

Captain Gray is remembered as a bold and able sea captain. He carried letters from President George Washington, Thomas Jefferson, and John Hancock on his journey to the Pacific, hand-written letters asking all leaders to receive him with kindness and treat him in a "becoming manner." He traveled fifteen miles up the river and traded with Native Americans for fur and salmon—he offered nails and sheets of copper and cloth on behalf of his benefactors, a group of eastern merchants. He then traveled to China, where he made a fortune selling the furs for one hundred dollars each.

Almost two decades after Captain Gray discovered the mouth of the river (the old-growth trees on our land were then entering adolescence), David Thompson of the Northwest Company of Merchants of Canada stood at the headwaters on Columbia Lake, the first white man to see the origin of the Columbia River. These two men were the bookends of discovery, one by sea and one by land, and with their respective claims the building of the Pacific Northwest began. From Canada's Columbia Lake, the river flows 1,200 miles to the western sea—500 miles in Canada and 700 miles in the United States. The river drains 259,000 miles in two countries and seven states, and is capable of providing one-third of the hydroelectric energy possible on the North American continent. Stuart Holbrook's statement in his classic book, *The Columbia,* says it all: "In the matter of fall and force, which is to say power, the Columbia stands alone in North America. Perhaps it stands alone anywhere."

Between my home in the Wallowa Mountains of eastern Oregon and my parents' home on the edge of the Cascades, there are now dozens of cities, a four-lane freeway through mountain ranges, a nuclear weapons facility, three dams, and several bridges that span the mighty Columbia. Needless to say, the river basin is well developed. During the first hundred years after discovery by the white men, pioneers dreamed, traveled, settled, and farmed near the river; during the second hundred years, scientists and developers learned to harness the power, and the river became a workhorse for industry.

In the time it took for the seedling to grow into our grandmother tree, pioneers have tamed a wilderness, conquered an ancient people, gentled a mighty river, employed weapons of mass destruction, doubled life expectancy, traveled to the moon, and gazed beyond. In the time it took for the seedling to grow, millions of trees have been logged and milled, thousands of animals have become extinct, dozens of wars have been fought and lost. In the time it took for the tree to grow, ten billion people have lived and died and one hundred billion have grieved their loss. If only my grandmother tree could talk.

When I walk the trails of my wilderness home and stand beside the old-growth trees, time occupies space in my mind, embodied in great towers of evolution that record two hundred years of incredible change. An old-growth tree is living history: Ring after ring was formed while the land was discovered, conquered, and almost destroyed, perhaps many times, the angels might tell us. And somewhere on the outer edge is a ring that was formed the year my mother was born, and each of the sixty-nine rings from then until now corresponds to events in her life. I could find a ring that was exposed to air the year my mother's mother died.

The tree captures time in a measure of rings, while my mother captures time through a legacy of love—invisible rings of human relationship that form the reality of her being. Perhaps my mother is much like the tree: Her history is hidden by an outer shell that covers the trauma and trial, and her strength is formed by layers of living, one upon the other.

The grandmother tree will sway in the wind until the final storm. And then, one autumn day, we'll discover a great root ball torn from the ground and branches the size of surrounding trees scattered across an acre of land. We'll trim the limbs, saw the trunk into rounds for firewood, burn the slash, and the grandmother tree will disappear from the land as if it had never been. I guess there is one difference between a tree and a person: The legacy of human love survives the original form, while a tree is harvested and forgotten.

When I walk the trails of my wilderness home, my mind is occupied by metaphor. I hear familiar emotion in the sound of the streams—lately they rage, but more often they coo and laugh; I find a comforting strength in the towering trees—their deep roots and open arms call to me; I discover a part of my origin in the instincts of the animals—in form and function we are much alike. But my history is unique and my destiny exists beyond this world. For now, I will root myself firmly in the soil of my wilderness home, enjoy my beloved mother and remember her life: a legacy of love sure to survive long after her ashes return to the land. And I will marvel at the strength of the human spirit and know that all good things will come to pass, perhaps some of them in the next two hundred years.

If only my grandmother tree could talk, perhaps we'd hear her say "Love well, child of man, for your life on this world passes quickly." Good advice from a tree. Now, if only the river could talk.

Thanks for your encouragement, Harry. I send gratitude for your friendship, as usual.

Love,

Janet

MAY 23, 1996

Angelkeep

Dear Harry,

There are times when my role as a mother becomes entangled with my role as a daughter, and I find myself sorting the needs of my growing children from those of my aging parents—"the big squeeze" I've heard it called. This is such a time.

My mother's suicide threat has made me wonder whether my parents should watch the girls while Keith and Michael travel to

Georgia for his brother's wedding in a couple of weeks. You and I and the rest of the planning team will be in Flagstaff finalizing the details of the international conference, so neither Keith nor I can be home with the children.

I think it's interesting, Harry, that the theme of our conference is "Living Faith." I find myself pondering the theme while addressing the specific questions raised by Mom's erratic behavior. Should we leave the girls despite her present emotional state? Should we risk the children remembering their grandmother surrounded by an angry cloud?

I called home a few days ago to express our concern: "Maybe we should revise our plans?" I asked gently.

"No," my mother said. "I'm fine, really." And my father felt he could care for the children without difficulty. "I think it's important that your mother have something to look forward to," he said repeatedly. "The girls will be my responsibility."

My father seems to have finally realized what a treasure the children are. During most of his adult life he refused to pay attention to little people until they could engage in political discussions; his mind subdued his heart. Now, however, he cherishes every hug and half-formed word, and finds great pleasure preparing strawberry waffles for their breakfast. I know these tendencies have always resided within my kindhearted father, but the trappings of his gender muffled their call. The miracle of our generation is that men no longer believe relationships are the domain of women. My father's generation came to this realization late, after the children were raised and launched; now they play catch-up with grandchildren. But the joy my father brings to the task is unparalleled, so we decided to leave the children despite some hesitation.

And my mother needs one last opportunity to care for her grandchildren. She seems to be working hard to present herself as a thriving woman and a supportive mother. "When the girls come" is now a frequent refrain, and she talks of preparing a playroom for my daughters complete with jewelry and the fancy clothes she no longer needs. She has always been a loving grand-mother, although not always a willing caretaker—once a year she watched the children when called upon, but she never volunteered. An occasional visit between cards and phone calls satisfied Mom and I understood: Twenty-five years raising three children alone while my father worked out of town was enough child care, and she retired years ago. After they bought the motor home and started traveling south every fall, their time at home gradually diminished; our last Christmas together was seven years ago. Needless to say, next weekend my parents will have a holiday with the children to make up for lost time, past and future.

My mother has finally learned to enjoy life, to harvest treasures in her final years. She and Dad have made many new friends among the retired middle class, cultivating relationships under the warm sun of the Arizona winter. My parents have learned to dance, to golf, to sing, and to live together in peace. And now that Mom has returned home for her final months, snowbird friends are even more of a treasure. Many send cards and a few stop by to visit on their way north for the summer. Most know she will likely die before the next southern migration brings the flock together again—she and a few unknown others who will also enter the molting season. These people understand the inevitability of death.

Keith and I picked morel mushrooms yesterday, walking far up the mountain to hunt a wilderness treasure. Morels have a distinct cone-shaped cap, brown and shriveled like brains, and they taste sensational when cooked with a little maple syrup and soy sauce—my secret recipe. Mushroom buyers park dented trucks in abandoned gas stations and advertise with handwritten signs to buy the local crop for five dollars a pound. We hear they pay one hundred dollars for every pound of morels in Japan, but we pick only for pleasure and feel like children on an Easter egg hunt when we spy a big one beneath the matted grass.

The weather was unsettled, sending us under the cover of trees to escape sudden snow flurries, and then teasing us to the meadow with glorious sun. A few of the nursery flowers were moved indoors because of cold morning frost, and my strawberry plants—although thriving in their new bed—have yet to bloom. The only reason I mention my late bloomers is because many of the strawberries on the mountainside have flowered already, wild plants with little white tops that will soon be crushed underfoot by the hunters—or if not crushed, their small hard berries will be devoured by predators before they are ripe. Unlike morel mushrooms—treasures that rise to peak form in the wilderness—strawberries grow better with cultivation; in mid-July I'll make a pie with the sweetest berries known to man, or beast.

Dad's love is like a morel mushroom that rises in spring without fanfare, a treasure uncultivated and unmatched; Mom's love is like a mountain strawberry that improves with cultivation, a sweet pleasure worth the work. The growing season has been long and hard, but the love my parents offer my children has risen to full height and is fully ripe. I only hope the weather holds.

The potential for trauma will tug at me, and I won't relax without a finger raised to test my mother's emotional wind. Frequent phone calls, secret backup plans, and prayers are my defense—part of the reason I asked you to stay for all the meetings in Flagstaff, Harry, which I appreciate greatly. But the decision for young and old to spend the weekend together is the best for all concerned: My parents need to be fully functioning grandparents one last time, and my children need to reap the harvest of love they offer. And I need to let go—to let love grow like nature intends. There is, after all, a season for everything.

With loving regards,

Janet

UNE 3, 1996

Angelkeep

Dear Harry,

To realize living faith in human life is not a simple matter. It starts with the challenge to find faith, then requires a decision to choose faith, and finally a meeting with the inevitable test: Can this faith be lived? Two days before I left for Flagstaff, my father's heart began to race, a medical emergency requiring quick decisions; another test of my faith.

At first I failed. I overreacted when Dad's cardiologist called Keith from the office as a courtesy and told him that a heart procedure had been scheduled for Thursday—the day I needed to leave for Flagstaff. Without consulting my parents I found alternative care for the girls and broke the news to Mom over the phone before Dad had even returned from the doctor's office. He was crestfallen, she told me later, when he heard the children weren't coming; he had rescheduled the procedure for the following Tuesday in order to care for them. The doctor explained the risks of delay, but my father was determined.

Which prompted my own soul search: Can I move forward without fear? My challenge was not whether to leave the children for the weekend—the needs of my parents outweighed the moderate risk—but how to do so with faith, to feel secure in the midst of compounded uncertainty. Yes, Keith and I decided after some discussion, we can do this.

Mom complained bitterly of pain when we arrived in The Dalles, pain that medication could not mask without diminishing her presence of mind, pain that the doctors could do nothing about. I noticed her angry set of jaw and trembling lips and narrowed eyes when I sat down—and said a prayer. The girls did not seem to notice, which concerned me even more: How would I know if they were being traumatized by the difficult side of the dying process? I wondered. But in the very next moment she spoke to the children in the most loving voice I have ever heard. Her strength of will transcended the fire of pain, and she moved from anger to love in a nanosecond.

Dad insisted on carrying my bags and then sat down, winded. I was torn between treating him like an invalid and trusting that for once he knows his limits. I decided to travel a middle ground: I carried my own bags but followed his instructions regarding cheap gas and free parking exactly (and I mean exactly) as they were offered. My father has been schooling me in the art of saving money since childhood, but I rarely passed his tests because for me time has more value than money. The savings amounted to seven dollars on gas and twenty dollars on parking, I was happy to report upon my return. Pretty good, Dad said.

After the weekend the girls seemed wound tight, as if the tension of disease and impending death had been silently absorbed without understanding or release, but they hugged my folks repeatedly and said, "Thanks for the great stuff." They were decked out with jewels from my mother's collection and more than ready to travel home. Both my parents looked really tired. Even so, Dad seemed impatient for conversation, holding medical pamphlets outlining code status and pacing around the garage while I loaded clothes and toys into the Suburban; he wanted to carry a suitcase or two, but I moved so quickly, he missed every chance.

Before leaving I wished him luck and told Mom to call from the hospital, but I should have stopped long enough to give him more emotional support. Something like "Are you scared?" would have opened the door to more meaningful conversation, the kind you end with a soft voice because the words are so hard: "Well, if anything happens, just know I love you, Dad. And don't worry; I'll take care of Mom." I dread to think that such a mad dash could be our last visit in earthly form. If this is true, I'll be sorely disappointed until I see him in the next world.

Tomorrow the doctors at Good Samaritan Hospital will thread a small catheter through the main artery that starts in my father's groin and runs to his heart. They expect to see a damaged heart muscle, perhaps a blocked artery, and who knows what else. My mother will rest in the waiting room until Dad is strong enough to travel to a nearby apartment they have borrowed from a friend. I have faith that everything will turn out all right, and that the kindness of friends—and angels—will see them through these difficult times. Mom has always said that every kindness is returned tenfold, and I believe she speaks the truth. The angels have been keeping track a long while and will surely return to my parents the kindness they have so faithfully earned.

As I drove along the Columbia River on my way home, I placed my parents in the angels' hands, knowing they would administer my own ration of kindness as only angels can. I discovered once again that living faith leads to a peaceful heart—within a few seconds every fear disappeared.

It was great to see you in Flagstaff, Harry. Plans for the conference are progressing well. I've come to believe that the more challenges we face, the better work we do. And besides, we're never given more difficulty than we can handle, the wise ones tell us. This truth is becoming self-evident.

With love and gratitude, as usual,

Janet

UNE 5, 1996

Angelkeep

Dear Harry,

Yesterday was a tough day for my mom. While she was waiting for Dad in the recovery room, she was told her brother-in-law had just died of cancer; he was diagnosed and dead within three months. When Joyce, Mom's older sister, came to nurse her after the second round of chemotherapy last March, she said her husband seemed increasingly distant and listless. When she returned home from helping Mom, she took him in for a checkup and the doctors found cancer in both of his lungs.

This is the second husband Joyce has lost to cancer. The first was thirty-six years old when he died, and because he was young and strong, the dying took a long time. When he screamed with pain, the sisters and brothers held him down until the morphine arrived; Mom said each couple took a shift to spare Joyce the sight of her lover in such agony. Death has punctuated my aunt Joyce's life: She was nine when her mother died of pneumonia; thirty-three when her first husband suffered beyond all reason; forty-nine when her teenage son was killed in a traffic accident; seventy-one now and widowed again.

Our two families have grown distant with time. Before Joyce remarried, she converted to a new religion and soon after traveled abroad on missionary work with her second husband and her children. The specifics of their theology made communication with those not of the faith more difficult, although my mother always stayed in touch—she refused to let differences stand in the way of their relationship. Religion, as I've said before, was a topic these sisters did not discuss.

The arbitrary dos and don'ts of religion—superstition and opinion enforced as creed—have always turned me off. But I've learned that religionists grow spiritually despite the trappings of religion. My aunt Joyce is a case in point: I saw her at a wedding a few years back, and we talked of various inconsequential things. Her graceful presence was like a gentle river and her radiant love like a winter sun, thawing my frozen perceptions upon first glance—an amazing lesson about the diverse roads we take to the same destination. My mother and father will travel to Hank's funeral on Saturday. If I happen to be in The Dalles when Aunt Joyce visits my mother, I can ask about her life: Did her wisdom rise from suffering? Does she look beyond religion now? Perhaps she always did; perhaps the problem was mine alone.

Mom is suffering more. There are open sores on her chest, and she has given up the fight against sleep-inducing medication; pain has won. She sounds drowsy and hoarse on the phone. Keith worried when he heard her speak because there's a nerve that can affect the vocal cords when invaded by cancer cells. Harry, my instinct is she'll go quickly now, but I must cease wondering how much time—two months, six months, twenty days—and prepare to care for her until the end. The anticipation is what challenges me; the actual nurturing is second nature, or maybe even first.

The children are out of school and the weather is beautiful. Between frequent trips to see my mother, I mow lawns, water gardens, and feel profoundly peaceful, even joyful. Not from my own mind, I want to say, but why try to describe in words what defies logic—I feel ready to face whatever comes. I hope I can bring this feeling to my mother's bedside when I see her next week, or that she finds it within herself eventually.

Regarding my father's health: He has a blocked artery they plan to open with angioplasty and a stent; the procedure is scheduled for Tuesday in Portland. I find it interesting that his heart condition is an "oh, by-the-way" kind of difficulty. If Mom were well, we'd be on Dad like bees on honey, telling him the dos and don'ts of repentance and recovery. But now it seems impending death is the status quo, and family life follows its own course regardless of what we do.

I heard that he repeatedly called the cardiac nurse "warden" yesterday. My dad will use his dry sense of humor all the way to the grave. Remind me of that when I bury him, Harry; a lifeline of humor may save me from the depths of despair. A few months ago

I made a bold prediction that he wouldn't suffer like Mom, that his heart would simply stop one day, maybe one day soon, given his physical appetites. Last night Dad announced that he plans to prove me wrong—he plans to live a long while and create lots of chaos in the years to come. He was teasing me and offering hope in the same breath. What a guy.

Mushroom season is over, and summer weather has finally arrived. Imagine watching baseball at a Little League field facing a ring of mountains capped with snow. A gentle breeze cools the family members sitting on wood bleachers, and as the innings pass, the sun sets behind the mountains, bathing the western sky with quickly changing colors. My son plays first base, and after struggling for eight years, now starts every game and bats number four in the line-up—the cleanup hitter. There must be a pleasure center for baseball in my brain, developed over the course of my adolescence in The Dalles—a true baseball town with long dry summers and a cool river wind, a farm town with a semipro team of handsome big brothers who always came home to play on school breaks. I traveled with the team as statistician the summer before I left home for college, a wild time filled with growing pains and a great love for the game.

When I first moved to The Dalles in seventh grade, I was very thin and equally shy, with imaginary illnesses and emotional outbursts. Nevertheless, in ninth grade I made the cheerleading team and by senior year was chosen captain. At first I was a bundle of bones and flesh flailing around, a sight to behold, but after relent-less practice I did the best job possible with ninety pounds of thin appendages; my friends called me "Stick." No one in my family played or even watched sports, so the evolution from cheerleader to statistician to mother of a good first baseman is an accomplish-ment. But the greatest accomplishment is that my son enjoys the game despite his mother's obsession.

All the twelve-year-olds who play Little League baseball around here will be considered for the all-star team that will represent our county during the district tournament in Burns this summer. If Michael makes the team, my life will be further complicated, but I would not deny him the opportunity to succeed; after eight years going to every possible practice and game, half the time sitting on the bench, the payoff for hard work is important for us both. And maybe I'm finding vicarious satisfaction from a son's accomplish-ment for reasons that have nothing to do with baseball.

When Michael was born, I held the small froglike boy and prayed to keep him, an irrational fear related to my status as a single mother and the threat of SIDS. Now he's beginning to look like a man, with broad shoulders and thick legs. Raising this child has been a challenge, and at times we were children together—many times. But there is gold at the end of the rainbow, and light all the way. Through the years I have waited patiently for encouragement to yield fruit, waited for the thud of a well-caught ball or the crack of a bat, waited for a child to blossom standing next to a canvas bag on a hot summer day, waited for an unfolding of a knowing: With enough time all things are possible. This might have been hard to believe watching me jump and flail in ninth grade, or watching Michael drop ball after ball through the years. But all things are possible, I tell myself when I sit on those wood bleachers and watch my son at first base; all good things are possible in time.

Time is what I give my parents, a valuable commodity when facing mortality. Mom says she has nothing left, but after forty years she and I are all-stars in the game of relationships and we do have time for one more inning; perhaps we'll count blessings and tally up scores. Once a statistician, always a statistician.

Enjoy your weekend, my friend. I'll stay in touch, as usual.

With love,

Janet

JUNE 11, 1996

Angelkeep

Dear Harry,

In two hours the doctors will once again thread a small device through my father's artery, inflate a balloon, remove a dam of plaque that has narrowed the flow of blood by 85 percent, and position a small coil of copper wire to keep the channel open; a routine procedure if all goes well. If not, the decrease in blood flow will damage the landscape of his body—the tissues and organs will suffocate, and my father will slowly turn to dust.

The Columbia River has had similar difficulties in its history. Tens of thousands of years ago, during the end of the last Ice Age, an ice dam blocked the regular channel the river followed through the northern plateau east of the mountains, and a bypass was forged nearby. When the ice melted, the river returned to its original course but left a deep coulee—a dry riverbed—one thousand feet to the bottom in a few places, and fifty miles long: the Grand Coulee. A waterfall at the south end of the plateau once dropped the full flow of the Columbia River 430 feet to the valley below; the sheer cliff, now called Dry Falls, is considered one of the wonders of the geologic world.

"Impressive" thought those who viewed the Grand Coulee from the edge of a two-million-acre wasteland; "intriguing" thought those who wanted to farm the rich and waterless land beyond the Columbia; "invaluable" thought those who fought and labored thirty years to build a dam that would once again fill the coulee with water.

The Grand Coulee Dam was completed in 1942, and the statistics reported in the press of the day were staggering: The dam created a 151-mile lake that submerged eleven towns; the dam rose twice as high as Niagara Falls and stretched so far that all the buildings of Rockefeller Center could sit on the spillway with three acres left for sale; the dam claimed the lives of more than eighty men who labored there but eventually supplied 60 percent of the power for the production of Allied planes and, therefore, won the Second World War for the American people. Actually, others would argue that it was the Hanford project, one hundred miles away by power line, that won the war.

As soon as the dam was complete, the military condemned 440,000 acres downstream and evicted 2,000 landowners to accommodate a secret project. They needed water, open spaces, and an exceptional amount of power to produce something the angry locals only understood after two explosions killed hundreds of thousands of people in Japan: the atomic bomb. The water used to cool the reactors was dumped in the Columbia for many years, and those of us who lived downwind and played in the river are now considered "at risk" for cell damage from radiation, a legacy shared with the Japanese.

The upside of the dam is that irrigation converted millions of acres of desert into rich farmland and orchards—the production of fruit and wheat in the area rivals that of any place in the world. Of course, progress brings unforeseen challenges: The many pesticides used to produce the wonderful fruits and grains we all consume have found their way to the river as well. Just this month a study was published—the first of its kind—that evaluates the health of the lower Columbia River and indicates that fish, wildlife, and those of us at the top of the food chain are ingesting unsafe levels of toxins. The fish are contaminated; the reproduction of eagles, badgers, and otters has been severely limited; and pregnant women are cautioned not to eat "an excess" of fish from the river. The higher the toxins rise in the food chain, the more concentrated and dangerous they become. The study urges caution and further study.

A few days after I received this study in the mail, the newspaper reported that a new study has taken the environmental scientists by complete surprise: The pesticides linked to breast cancer are one thousand times more dangerous in combination with one another than previous studies on individual toxins have indicated. The toxins elevate estrogen levels and besides causing breast cancer, stunt the development of male sex organs; the "combination effect" increases the risk of cancer beyond anyone's imagination. A dynamic discovery, it is fair to say: a hidden tax on progress.

Progress most likely caused the cancer that killed my uncle Hank in Richland, the city that Hanford spawned and that employed my uncle for many years. Progress most likely caused the cancer that will kill my mother in The Dalles, the city that rests on the banks of a river filled with contaminated fish she loved to eat. But progress most likely will save my father—his blood will flow without restriction for many years to come, we hope.

Like respiration, progress expands and contracts life in mysterious ways, filling us with hope and then killing a few with unexpected results, events that leave us breathless with fear and foreboding regarding what it is we might have done. Like respiration, there always seems to be a solution—another breath that brings another discovery—more progress and more unanticipated results.

There are times, however, when progress is pursued despite evidence of harm because the part refuses to consider the whole. The whole requires our attention now—the whole ecosystem, the whole family of humanity. The "combination effect" cannot be denied, and thus each part is responsible to the whole. We all breathe the same air, drink the same water, eat the same fish, pray to the same God.

My mother becomes hoarse with rage at incompetent doctors when pain exceeds her tolerance point. She blames the part but will find comfort only when she embraces the whole of her life—her relationships, her faith, her status as a child of God. She belongs to a vast and miraculous whole, an interconnected reality more diverse and dynamic than the world in which she lives, more dynamic than her most vivid dreams of heaven. Death is progress regardless of cause when viewed from a cosmic perspective: Mortal death leads to eternal life—another breath.

The children have given up waiting on me and are entertaining themselves out of doors, an indication of how long it takes to write these letters. Hope your vacation went well. I envision you walking through the mountain wildflowers and talking with your children; I'm off to play with mine, finally.

With loving regards,

Janet

J UNE 13, 1996
Angelkeep

Dear Harry,

Have you ever had a dream of reassurance, a dream where the counsel to "fear not" and the face of a loved one are merged in feeling, a dream from which you wake wondering if the angels have taken another soul to the next world? Last night I dreamed of my father several times, dreams of love that turned to fear upon the waking, an interpretation entirely too human. And now I long to hear his voice, but it's only 6 A.M., so I'll rest my emotions in a quickly fading dreamworld, and occupy my mind by writing you while the early side of the morning wanes.

My father's voice has been filled with pain the past few days, a sound unfamiliar and unnerving, the sound of a shadow reality moving to light: my father's mortality. The statistics reported by family members regarding Dad's health have always been impressive: He has never been sick, has never been in the hospital; has never taken the doctors' advice, has never complained of pain, smokes and drinks and eats with gusto—a self-reliant man with an iron constitution and a stubborn will. And now the stats have changed: suffered greatly with pain; stayed an extra day in the hospital; sits in the passenger seat; no fat, no cigars, no mowing the lawn—a physically humbled man with a damaged heart and a flood of new emotions.

Regardless of spiritual insight, facing mortality stirs deep fears and uncovers identity issues most of us thought were buried for good. My father's difficulty is an apt illustration: Physical strength, independence, and freedom have fled with his health, and the head of our family—my mother's caretaker—is temporarily forced to settle for infirmity, dependence, and the service of those who love him. A big switch for a generous man who has always been the one helping others. A big switch for a loving daughter who has always admired his strength. Now I must learn to relieve his pain without stealing his dignity and nurture his health without starving his character—a character formed of the habits, the history, the hidden fears that define my father's sense of self.

Facing the mortality of both mother and father has challenged my strength, Harry, as you might well imagine. My response to

Mom's illness evolved in steps, a series that can only be viewed as progress in retrospect. The first step was to imagine more than a few aches in my own body—to feel breast lumps and chest pains. Anxiety reared its ugly head in physical form, and I struggled to master myself. "Breathe deeply," I said when my chest felt incredibly tight. "Just another cyst," I reasoned when my breast felt lumpy and sore; maybe I pushed too hard.

The second step—once my aches and pains receded—was to dismiss my mother's pain, to separate myself from sympathy, to use the reality check as a whitewash—accept the facts, Mom—and then paint a spiritual picture across the flat canvas of her suffering. Unproductive, to say the least, since my mother has always depended on me to understand her pain.

The third and current step is to realize her pain is real and mine is not; my pain is a shadow of reality—a fear response.

Fear. Not something to dispatch with ease or with intellect it seems. I know that fear leads to pain and may cause disease. I know that fearlessness illuminates the shadows and illustrates the power of love. But knowing is not the same as doing I've learned more than once and am learning again: Knowing needs time to unfold, to dress itself in experience, to bring itself to the table as a reality and not simply a goal. I've held a variety of goals a long while—to interpret without prejudice, to understand without judgment, to love without hesitation, to live without fear—and now finally understand that realizing these goals may take an eternity, even with the help of reassuring dreams.

Perhaps my fourth step should be to live without fear one day at a time—to be satisfied with the current step, however small.

My parents called from the hospital room to say the surgery went well. My dad sounded stronger and spoke with less pain in his voice. Mom has arranged for transportation, housekeeping, and meals for the next few days; I will take over their care next Tuesday. Now that Dad seems certain to survive, my dream of reassurance provides both inspiration and comfort. I remember it with gratitude.

Hope all is well with you, my friend. I'm sure you have many tasks at hand now that vacation is over—a few calls to make, a few letters to read.

Much love,

Janet

Summer

J UNE 24, 1996

Angelkeep

Dear Harry,

Fear and love define the spectrum of experience I shared with my parents last week, seven days filled with sudden storms, health scares, emotional release, chronic pain, pinochle games, and meaningful conversations: family relationships in classic form, dysfunction and all.

When I arrived, the battle of the wounds began. My father lowered his pants to show me the amazing bruise left on his thigh after the heart procedure, the result of clamps on flesh and blood seeping under skin. My mother opened her blouse and displayed weeping sores, a dozen of them, surrounded by red and swollen skin.

The first emotional storm arose within fifteen minutes. While my father and I were talking in the kitchen, the volume of the television program my mother was watching in the living room slowly increased; it was clear she wanted my attention and, like a child, escalated the noise until I responded. And then came her anger—intense and raw—the result of fear submerged in the midst of Dad's medical tests and the tension of the unknown, the result of pain ignored and the exhaustion of every step between the waiting room and my father's bedside, the result of grief denied and the dawning reality of her brother-in-law's death. Fear, pain, and grief poured from my mother in overwhelming waves of emotion. If we were going to ignore her, she yelled and cried at the same time, then she might as well die.

I struggled for control and then surrendered. "If you can get angry, then I can cry," I said with a smile while tears flowed, and Mom quickly settled down.

"I don't want to burden you, honey," she said, still flushed with the afterglow of rage. Our simultaneous purging of anger and tears opened a familiar channel of suffering between us, a channel we often travel these days, a channel of darkness that moves to light—a tunnel through rock.

The life cycle of the family unfolded before me as I comforted both mother and father. Their need for my presence reminded me of the hunger a young child feels for the mother: hunger for food and warmth, hunger for strength and security, hunger for a loving relationship with the other, and I was the other. I wanted to be the other, cherished the opportunity, and they knew. My mother held nothing back. She exhaled in true form her entire life: the trials and triumphs, the fear and love. My father walked slowly, stooped and grimacing, with gratitude for my presence in every glance.

I remembered to ask some of the questions, Harry, you encouraged me to ask: about her childhood, her marriage, her motherhood. The most meaningful conversation she started without any prompting. We talked about the anger a young child must feel for the death of a mother, an abandonment without fault and still filled with blame. She spoke for all the children who have lost mothers in the early years; she spoke for every child who finally realizes how significant the loss is after years of denial; she spoke for her own child trapped within who longs to forgive and be forgiven. She seemed willing to understand the depth of her pain for a few brief and beautiful moments, and I listened in silence while she forged a way home.

By instinct I discovered a great source of comfort for Mom: massage. I rubbed her feet, her hands, her head with the half inch of gray hair—a testimony to age and experience. With wig and bandanna aside, she looked like a victim in the classic sense: a round, almost bald head, with ashen skin and deep circles under tired eyes. With little effort I discovered the mother I knew beneath the physical trauma, but her form symbolized pain, Harry, and I grieved for her suffering within the deep and hidden recesses of my own being. I prayed and rubbed and hoped her pain would respond to the call of my loving fingers: release, release, release. And we tended to our grooming: clipped toenails, filed and polished fingernails, bleached her half inch of gray hair a nice copper blond. Like girls together, we embraced our material form and found true delight in the everyday rituals of the female gender, which is something I rarely do, something my mother has always wanted to teach me.

Comfort is strong medicine for Mother's emotional storms. Even though touch and tenderness did not end her outbursts, the intensity diminished more rapidly with each gentle stroke. Our constant and intimate contact with hands, heart, and mind composed a rhythm of fear and love; the rise and fall of emotion became our cadence.

The rapid onset of her anger Wednesday night took me by surprise, however, because of the lateness of the hour. It was almost midnight when she cranked up the Beach Boys to express the intensity of her rage, and I was tired. I polished the kitchen for another few minutes, asked politely about the fairness of her verbal attack on my father, and went to my room. A few minutes later I was relieved to hear my parents calmly talking about the quality of their companionship during forty-four years of a difficult marriage.

Before terminal illness, separate domains were a comfort to them both. Mom watched television upstairs while cooking and cleaning house, and Dad watched television downstairs while paying bills and smoking the forbidden cigar. Now she is desperate for company and complains about dying alone in the living room easy chair. The final days of their marriage needed negotiation. I was comforted by the love in their dueling voices and after a time rejoined them, said good night with hugs and kisses, and escaped the waking world with a peaceful heart; an accomplishment for us all.

Thursday morning we met with Hospice. A woman arrived

promptly at ten and introduced herself as Mom's nurse—the family doctor speculated that Mom would be dead within six months, thus confirming the need for hospice care. The three of us were taken aback by this open declaration of finality, but not surprised.

We sat in a circle of mixed chairs and talked for three hours; actually they talked and I asked a question every thirty minutes or so, questions like "How do you feel about all of this, Dad?" He answered me directly: "Like a failure."

With careful prodding he explained that he did, indeed, need help with the mechanics of her medical care; he could see the reality of terminal illness unfolding before him. But he was good at the mechanics of care, much better than he was with emotional comfort. Now it seemed that all her needs were beyond his skill.

He was honest about his feelings, and upset enough to send his blood pressure through the roof. The nurse confirmed it was over two hundred, the critical mark, but there was nothing we could do. The mechanics of his care escape me because they relate directly to lifestyle: what he eats, drinks, smokes; what he does and doesn't do. His life is not my job, I think to myself—a personal defense against failure. But perhaps I simply resist assuming the role my mother holds so lightly; perhaps a year from now I'll be giving advice with the best of them—if he still needs advice.

Harry, you asked if I think anger is a form of fear, and I have to say yes—anger, denial, blame, bravado all relate to an innate animal fear of death at the hands of the other. My mother vents her anger at God on occasion, a response to a fear more profound than all the rest: "He's punishing me!" she cries with red face and clenched teeth.

I have reframed my view of her anger, however. Before I saw a frightened child, a need to blame, a denial. Now I see a strong will, a need to live, a desperate embrace. A day may come in the near future when she'll have no strength for anger and no will to live, a day when I'll long for the intensity of emotion we shared, for her fear in all its challenging forms.

It was a long week, Harry, and many experiences will be remembered only in the fullness of time. She has decided that suicide would harm the children and is prepared to let the dying process take its own course; we'll have as many days together as her mortal form can muster.

The more I learn from this experience, the more reluctant I am to pray for the end. But the time will come when her death is awaited with anticipation, like the birth of a child; the time will come when we pray for my mother to live again in another form— another, more perfect form.

It was nice to talk with you on Sunday. As usual, I am grateful for our friendship.

With love,

Janet

JUNE 27, 1996

Angelkeep

Dear Harry,

A pair of lady's slippers is growing wild in the woods. Keith discovered them while checking the trout he stocked in two nearby ponds last month. The orchids have a delicate white boot below a yellow stamen and hang from a thin stalk surrounded by a dozen large leaves; they hang like shoes on display in the shade of the tall pines. Keith has built a fence around the flowers by stacking tree branches in a loose square, and the deer have spared them, which is amazing because they grow along the game trail the deer travel every evening to our almost-fenced garden.

I recognized the lady's slippers upon first glance even though I had never seen one—they are perfectly named. And rare around here; no one we talked with had ever seen one on the mountainside. I wonder how the flowers came to grow next to the pond: Did a bird transport the seed last year and plant the flower like nature intends? Or did the angels bring a gift?

Words cannot fully describe the experience of seeing these delicate orchids thrive in the wilderness. The one-inch white boot is gently curved, a slip-on of delicate lace. The yellow stamen is like a satin tongue, smooth and securely attached at the back of the boot. The entire flower is crowned by red petals that remind me of a jester's hat. Flat green leaves grow at various heights on a stem that rises ten inches above the forest floor. All around these two fragile flowers is a wild wood, with stinging nettles, falling branches, towering trees, rushing streams, and the remnants of a salt block knocked to the ground by a frisky deer. These rare treasures are the result of perfect conditions in the surrounding environment, a mystery or maybe an accident—or so it might seem to the dispassionate eye.

I wish my mother could see these orchids. She would understand with instinct what I have tried to explain with intellect and she has denied with emotion: In the midst of extreme conditions or intense transitions exceptional beauty can emerge—gifts buried in sacred ground like a flowering cactus in the desert, a delicate orchid in the wilderness, a meaningful relationship with a willing stranger.

There are strangers poised to help my mother, employees of Hospice trained to care for the dying. At first my mother refused their help and then reluctantly agreed to meet them once—only to satisfy requirements. The team consists of a social worker, a pastor, and a home health aide in addition to the nurse whom we have already met.

"Am I asking too much of my family?" Mom sobbed when we encouraged her to meet the team. "Why would I want strangers to do for me what family and friends should be doing?" Her clenched teeth warned of intense anger, but she needed the hospice team, so I decided to plead.

"It's not an either/or situation, Mom. You'll have the family and the hospice team both." I tried to reach her with reason, but emotion rose to her defense. Fear of the unknown presented a deep chasm between us that logic could not bridge.

I rose above logic and tried meaning: "We're all brothers and sisters, Mom. They would only be strangers for a moment and then friends, I'm sure; perhaps even exceptional friends."

And then I spoke with quiet passion because my arguments became more personal: "Helping someone through the dying process is a transforming experience, Mom. I'm growing stronger every day."

And she agreed. She told me that as a child I was the sick and contemplative type, rocking for hours and twisting my hair; my sister was more of a tomboy. Mom stopped for a minute and then corrected herself: "No, Janet, you were always strong. I just didn't know how strong."

"I'm strong now because I need to be, Mom," I said quietly. "I'm rising to the occasion for you like you have always risen for me."

Harry, I hold the hospice team members in awe, veterans of the dying process. I wonder if their transforming experience is accumulative. Do they become stronger every time they help someone die? Does their strength remain or fade after each death? It seems a great, sacred mystery to me, one that can be solved only with experience—the kind you have with your own mother, my friend.

With each passing day Mom's physical and emotional suffering intensifies. But we seem to find spiritual strength in direct proportion to suffering, as if by ascending the spiral of pain we rise to greater spiritual heights, like a delicate orchid rising from the rich soil of a wild wood.

Mom called today to say that since she always wins in pinochle, I was allowed to be right about something: She loves the hospice team members. And there are other understandings my mother discovers, brief and beautiful moments that come and go without fanfare. We travel sacred ground on this road to death, and each of us finds unexpected treasure: I find lady's slippers—spiritual meanings that rise from suffering; Mom finds comfort—loving relationships that rise from a stranger's embrace.

Hope all is well with you, my friend. Can't wait to see you at the conference in Flagstaff, only a month away.

With fondness and love,

Janet

JULY 1, 1996
Angelkeep

Dear Harry,

Death is all around us. The two little kittens we brought home to help reduce the mice population are now champion killers, and every day we find prized bodies and body parts on the workshop floor. They live in the workshop, sleep on an old couch, and bring gifts for the master to show their gratitude and prowess. Yesterday we found the head of a rabbit, two baby birds, two whole squirrels, and a shrew. We put collars and bells around their fat necks, but these cats are smart.

A few days ago, Keith was held spellbound by a screaming lecture from an angry squirrel—a resident who felt the garden should be off limits to humans—when Max pounced from the side and killed the squirrel in one swift move. Our family cat used his master for a decoy and then proudly ran to the workshop with a fresh corpse dangling from his mouth. There is little more we can do to stop these cats from killing the neighbors, so we make "Catkill Café" jokes and laugh to overcome our dismay at the strength of the killing instinct and the inevitability of death; we laugh to overcome our helplessness.

A deer ate one of the lady's slippers, so we may dig up the mate and try to cultivate orchids in the workshop; perhaps a bit of culture will tame our wild cats. I've developed a new interest in orchids, like others of my kind who have loved the flowers for their beauty and fragrance for thousands of years. In the seventeenth century hundreds of "company men" braved hostile seas and mysterious natives to dig up orchids in the jungle and transport them back to wealthy aristocrats in England, thus beginning the cultivation of orchids in Europe. One hundred years later, Charles Darwin discovered his theory of evolution as a result of his interest in the reproduction of orchids. I was fascinated to learn that the lady's slipper is a hybrid, the result of experiments in species modification. I would like to donate our two cats to this kind of research; perhaps the scientists can breed a cat that will kill only mice.

I find great comfort in humor, Harry, a gift unique to the human being. We hold fear in common with other animals, but none acquire the wisdom to laugh. Humor is one of the great tools we use to overcome fear, to help us transcend the animal nature and develop our humanity, to build a bridge between pain and joy. And herein lies the ultimate joke: Evolution from the material to the spiritual requires that we laugh at ourselves. What a design.

My mother struggles to find humor these days. She and I used to laugh over silly mistakes, somehow finding great humor in the mundane; we used to laugh so hard that tears would roll down our cheeks and the mistake was forgotten in the catharsis. People would watch for several minutes and finally ask, "What's so funny?" We would look at each other, puzzled because we couldn't remember, and then begin our hysterics again. What remains of our humor is a treasure these days—a reminder of how best to handle fear, of how far we've come, and of how strong we can be in the face of impending death.

My mother called yesterday in tears, ready to pack and escape to the nearest hotel. Weekends at home without company are especially hard; even her "friends" on the weekday soaps desert her. My father is increasingly tired and falls asleep in the chair downstairs, leaving my mother to flip channels and build anger upstairs. My challenge this month is time, especially now that Michael has made the all-star team; he will practice every night for two weeks and then attend a three-day district tournament on the far side of the state in July. I'm not sure when I can return to The Dalles. The only option is for Mom to come here, and after several heated discussions she agreed to rent the cabin down the road for a couple of nights. She worries about the altitude, but next to the pain and suffering of cancer, I told her, the altitude sickness will pale.

I'm planning to laugh a lot while she's here, to find humor in life and transcend the suffering if possible. If not, maybe the cats will deliver a feast for the café and I can eulogize dead rodents with wild stews and soufflés. As they say, we're in this soup together and a little humor in the face of death might just be the perfect seasoning.

I hope you're finding humor in your own challenging life, my friend.

With love,

Janet

JULY 3, 1996

Angelkeep

Dear Harry,

When my parents arrived at the ball field last night, we were all pushed to the limit. Michael was sore and exhausted after finishing a grueling three-hour practice with his new military-type coach; I was sore and exhausted after spending the day cleaning two cabins in addition to my other work; my folks were sore and exhausted after driving five hours without a break. But their timing was perfect, and without hesitation they counseled Michael on the benefits of being pushed to the limit: exercise for both body and mind.

We all felt uplifted after a few minutes of companionship. There is no better way to deal with your own difficulties than to help someone else with theirs. I took a little longer to unwind because my difficulty stemmed from having too many people to help. Mom turned into a military-type mother when we arrived at the rental cabin, and pointed to the chair by the tall glass windows overlooking the forest. "Sit!" she ordered, and I did.

Too much or too many is not really an accurate description of my stress—I resist thinking my life could hold more than I can handle. Feeling overwhelmed is caused by a lack of organization, I tell myself, and having unfinished work when new tasks arise. By nature I am a linear being: first this, then that. Life, however, requires that I embrace the whole: All of these tasks are related to the ultimate purpose, the evolution from the material to the spiritual.

Lately the "all of these" consists of unfinished projects hurtling to conclusion; my stress comes from juggling diverse parts while trying to keep an eye on the whole. I counsel myself to open like a flower and embrace all of life, to breathe deep from the well of universe energy, to exhale with intention and grace. And then I feel better, I know that everything required will be provided—has already been provided—and I give thanks.

It's the giving thanks part that is so difficult for Michael— he cannot fathom speaking to his new coach by choice, let alone thanking him. But I smile and say, "Well, Michael, this kind of experience makes a good story—the triumph of the human spirit in the midst of what seems like an overwhelming challenge." He can relate to a good story because he reads hundreds of novels. "Rise to the challenge," I say, and imagine him the hero in a "Monster Coach

Molds Winning All-Star Team" paperback just for kids like him.

I want to say the same thing to Mom but hold the words in my heart instead; she seems so fragile, so brittle from pain. And all the advice from the most wise in this world won't help her learn to rise and flower. These are lessons for her next life, a life that begins without heart-wrenching memories, without guilt and blame.

Imagine waking without the hidden reservoir of pain all human beings carry; imagine waking with a new form and realizing that lost mothers and fathers, sisters and brothers, children, friends, and lovers still walk somewhere in the same universe; imagine waking to your own eternal life. She will rise and flower then, I'm sure.

In the meantime she clings to suffering and recites a litany of misdeeds and mistakes as if her rationale for anger resides in the words. And I want to shout, "Forgive! Let the pain and sorrow fade into oblivion; let the joy of eternity illuminate the final road you travel in material form." Perhaps I will tomorrow.

Thanks for your encouragement, my friend. Regardless of the challenges, I feel blessed by friends and family.

With fondness and love,

Janet

ULY 6, 1996

Angelkeep

Dear Harry,

Many years ago a large pine fell in the forest and a ten-foot section was cut and planed to bridge a stream. I found my way to this peaceful spot recently when my emotions rose to the surface and carried me away. Watercress lined the stream that flowed beneath me; a beautiful place to cry, I thought, as tears fell and merged with springwater. I watched tall grass gently sway, butterflies move from flower to flower, and water race through green banks— water that has most likely traveled around the world a million times or more already. The water seemed wise to this weary traveler, and I thought of the truth Siddhartha discovered in the peaceful flow of a stream at his feet. I remembered to keep my own counsel: to gather strength from the source, to live with assurance and faith. Comforting words similar to those the sage must have heard in the quiet of his own willing mind, in the dance of water over stones: Breathe deeply, child.

My counsel to Mother caused a crisis. For once I resisted her anger and blame, suggested forgiveness, encouraged her to depend on faith, and then watched the tempest rise in response.

"You were the last understanding person in the world," she said as her pain emerged in emotional form.

"Without faith, Mother, you have no defense against the suffering," I said, and rubbed her feet while she tried to explain how the pain influences her mind. She worries the cancer has found her brain and destroyed her faith; she doesn't know what to believe anymore.

"And besides," she cried with emotion again, "hundreds of prayers go unanswered while the cancer rages. God doesn't care about me."

Once again we found our way to the fundamental issue in my mother's life, and mine for that matter. Can we forgive in the midst of pain? Can we suffer and love simultaneously? The woman who taught me this lesson has failed to learn it herself, which is one of the strange but true realities of relationships: We teach best what we most need to learn. The concepts of sin and suffering are fully entwined in my mother's mind—one begets the other. I have tried to help her understand that suffering is a natural and necessary part of mortal existence, an element in the evolution from the material to the spiritual, the leverage that motivates personal progress, but she is filled with blame and shame and believes she deserves to be punished for her mistakes. God cares only for the righteous while she is allowed to suffer. He has deserted her, just like her mother deserted her.

And I argued the opposite, of course. But Mom adopted

her rationale for suffering long before I was born, and there are few words able to change such a fundamental assumption once a life is built around it. I have tried and failed many times.

After our brief and emotional conversation she finally went back to her cabin, weak and weary from the battle between body and mind and wondering, I hope, about faith and forgiveness.

The next morning she rose late from bed. The inflammation spreading across her chest was swollen and so painful she cried for relief: "Why can't anyone help me?" Keith tried to help, but all he could do was confirm the suggestions of salves and bandages she had already tried. The choice between continued experimentation or increased medication enraged her.

"So, I'll just go home, take a few more pills, climb in bed, and die," she said. The two-hour scene that followed covered the entire spectrum of human pain, and at one point everyone was crying except for me. I cried later, on the bridge.

Mom knows her rage hurts other people, especially my dad. Last night they shared the same bed for the first time in several months. Dad sat upright four times and asked in a panic, "What's wrong, Marian? What's wrong?" Mom had been sleeping soundly. Because she feels helpless to control her anger, she promised once again to take Valium with the morphine. The pills may help her more than my advice regarding forgiveness, although like our good friend Steve says, the more fuss people make after hearing advice, the more likely they are to follow it.

I felt the need to apologize for some unknown reason, but Mom wouldn't hear of it. "Remember the famous line in *Love Story*, Janet: 'Love means never having to say you're sorry.'" And so we made a deal not to apologize to each other. I finally understand what that line actually means: no blame or guilt when things get tough. The movie wife who made that statement was also dying of cancer.

Even though I understand, Harry, I don't agree. An apology sometimes helps the one who feels helpless, who watches the suffering and can do nothing but rub feet and talk of heaven, who needs to say "I'm sorry" and kiss the beloved on a pale and wrinkled brow. I am truly sorry for her suffering.

That evening I brought lasagna for dinner and played pinochle with Mom on the bed. Even though her face was round and puffy, her gray-copper hair stood on end almost an inch, and her chest was exposed and bleeding, we played as if nothing in the world mattered but who took the bid. Life seems quite normal when we shuffle and deal and pray for a good hand. Every game starts with hope, every hand holds the possibility of something new, and therein lies the beauty of the game: Hope is easy to sustain when the next hand is just around the corner. I wish Mom could believe in her next life as easily as she can her next hand; I wish she was willing to look around the corner. And she wishes that I lived around the corner, that we could share dinner and a game of cards every night.

When I phoned to see if they arrived home safely, Mom was upset again. I offered to call twice a day, to pretend I lived around the corner, and she seemed to settle down. My relationship with Mom is unique, I realize. During our last conversation we talked of the next life and what happens when the sleeper arises. "Does the anticipation of seeing your mother bring you comfort, Mom?" I asked.

And she answered with a truth that has never been spoken aloud: "I don't know her, Janet. You are more of a mother to me."

I am my mother's mother, just as I am my brother's keeper. The accidents of birth have been erased by time—the daughter becomes the mother and the mother becomes the child. Although my mother and I have always traded roles, as I mentioned before, her acknowledgment of our unique exchange strengthened me.

My dad seems so tired, I would like to parent him as well. But I hold a vision of him standing on the deck of their rented cabin one sunny morning when I arrived with the children: He waved and smiled like he had not a care in the world but to visit with us. He will survive the trauma of Mom's difficult dying; we all will—even Mom.

It is a marvelous day on the mountain, Harry. I am planning to take the children to the lake and bask in the beauty of this challenging world. Thanks for listening, my friend.

With love,

Janet

Dear Harry,

Last night I suddenly woke from a peaceful sleep as if someone had tapped my mind and whispered, "Awake!" Although I seemed fully alert, my body did not stir. Outside the window a magnificent moon was cradled between two trees, a moon so bright and so full, it seemed to be perched on the windowsill, peering in. Oh, what a beautiful moon, I thought, and then gently drifted back to sleep, filled with gratitude for such a wonderful sight.

This morning I checked the lunar calendar and found we are two days beyond the last quarter moon—a full moon was impossible. Was I dreaming? I can't comprehend how such a vivid image could be a dream, but the calendar does not lie—does my mind? I was surely conscious, even though my body slept.

The moon was the second incredible beauty I saw last night; the first was the sunset. I was driving west through the valley along high peaks and green fields, when I was dangerously distracted by a stunning vista: The mountain ridge—with ribbons of white snow still snaking down crevices—was glowing red from behind. Above the ridge a few brush strokes of dense clouds were blended a deep violet, the result of moisture and red light mixed with descending shadows.

Color moved from north and south along the horizon toward the setting sun, lighting the bottom edge of a long cloud with the same intense red that highlighted the top of the ridge. A cluster of clouds just above the disappearing sun glowed like fire in the sky. Rarely have I seen such intense color from a setting sun, or such bright light from a quarter moon. One was a wonder of nature, and the other, I believe, was a miracle of mind; both were gifts.

My mother receives gifts as well. She told me a story on the phone last night—another tale of rescue by friends. It was a difficult day, and Mom was planning an escape. She was packing her bag when the neighbors called with an invitation to a barbecue; they were good friends and both my parents were happy to accept.

Over the course of the evening the two women talked of their children—their daughters, Judy and Karen, had been best friends in high school. Suddenly, Mom's friend remembered the date: Nineteen years ago on this same July day Karen had been murdered. It was the anniversary of that heinous crime, the crime from which my sister has never recovered, the crime that brought these two women together.

Mom's friend told the story of her grief. Her daughter had been engaged and planning her wedding when she was abducted in a parking lot, driven out of town, and shot by a man who was visiting his own children; he was caught months later after bragging to a transient of his deed. The shock and fear was overwhelming for both families. Judy combed the surrounding hills for endless days and spent long nights waiting by the phone for some word of her friend, although foul play was suspected from the start: Karen was a happy young woman planning the rest of her life—she would not have disappeared by choice.

Mom's friend told of the darkness that followed, of the anger and pain that seemed to overwhelm her, making it impossible to work, to eat, to feel anything but grief. And then one night she had a dream: Karen stood at the foot of the bed, speaking an unknown language.

"I can't understand you, Karen," the mother said.

"I know, Mother," the daughter said, and smiled. "Let go."

From that night on Karen's mother was at peace. She knew the visit was a gift; she knew her daughter walked in another form, spoke in another language, lived in another—more perfect—world.

Mom told this story as a testimony to faith. Even though she has trouble finding her own in the midst of pain, she believes in the miracles, and in life after death. Stories of tragedy and triumph renew everyone's faith; they are the essence of life captured and distilled and shared as gifts in times of need—the living truth of a shared humanity.

Keith tells two stories from his family history that I place in the "miracles of mind" category. The first belongs to a distant relative who woke one night with a vision of a car accident, a fire, and his mother standing at the foot of the bed. She said, "Don't worry, son, I'll be all right." The next morning he learned that she had been involved in a fatal traffic accident the night before and the car had burned, killing her.

The other story comes from a well-loved grandfather. He and his mother had an uncanny connection: She always knew when something was wrong. One night he was patrolling a U.S. air base in France, where he was stationed during the war, when he noticed that an ammunitions pile was on fire and tried to put it out. That same night his mother had a dream that her son was standing at the foot of the bed in his flight suit; his arms were badly burned, but he was smiling. The son recovered and has told the story of his mother's vision, complete with scars, to every wide-eyed grandchild who would listen. They all listened well, especially Keith, who has told his grandfather's story to his own wide-eyed children on many occasions.

All three stories involve dreams of a loved one at the foot of the bed; all three are dreams of reassurance. I believe these dreams are miracles of mind, not supernatural events, a gift from the mind of God to the mind of the dreamer, a brief and miraculous merging with true mercy. And like those dreamers who found comfort from a visit at the foot of the bed, I will find comfort in the glow of the full moon—a vision, a miracle, a light for the road ahead.

Take care, Harry. Perhaps we'll have a chance to talk soon.

Love,

Janet

JULY 16, 1996

Angelkeep

Dear Harry,

Burns is a hot little town in southern Oregon where 150 young baseball players and their families gathered to live a dream: the Little League All Star Tournament. Keith and I traveled three hundred miles to watch Michael's team over the weekend, leaving our two girls with the cousins.

The largest motel in this depressed logging community burned to the ground last fall when a drug lab exploded, so accommodations were scarce. We stayed in the attic of a 1907 house that had been hastily converted into a bed-and-breakfast for the event, climbing steep stairs to a small apartment recently cleared of cobwebs and mice and stocked with packages of bear claws and orange juice, and the remnants of a library. The library was a treasure, with historical works on the Oregon Trail and a diverse collection of dated books filled with philosophy and metaphysics. We slept in twin beds under a hot breeze manufactured by little white fans that were clipped to the nightstand; the attic was like an oven due to day-time temperatures that were extreme even for a desert town.

Regardless of the heat, we enjoyed our time in Burns, spending long unscheduled hours in a hot attic talking philosophy and religion with friends, watching championship baseball from our lawn chairs by the first baseline fence, and spending more long hours in a cool tavern playing pool while songs from the seventies filled the air—a wonderful time warp back to our college days.

The ballplayers stayed with host families, so we had little opportunity to visit with Michael during the tournament. The coach rotated every player on the team through the lineup except Michael; he sat on the bench both games—the only child who did not have a chance to play. My heart breaks for my son. He dedicated his tournament play to his grandmother and promised to give her his game shirt when he returned. He even picked her favorite number to wear on his shirt—Lucky Seven—the name Mom picked for the boat Dad bought with her one and only jackpot.

During the past two weeks of exhausting practice and a raging coach, I have counseled Michael to return good for evil, to consider the challenges the coach faces in his own life, to remember this man works the graveyard shift at the mill and then drives to the ball field every day to coach the team as a volunteer. I assured Michael that the accomplishments of eight years cannot be erased by the experience of one tournament, one team, one coach. I challenged Michael to view the experience as a part of the whole, one unfortunate lesson in an eternity of learning. But I must confess, Harry, I feel angry and frustrated despite all my good advice.

Keith and I returned home before the tournament ended, leaving Michael to face this challenge alone. And now his understanding of the world expands to include a philosophy of winning at any cost, a psychology of punishing weakness, a sociology of bullies and the abuse of power. When he returns, we'll discuss the reality of undeserved suffering, and the spectrum of potential responses from which he must choose—hopefully, anger and frustration will not be his choice.

Michael called from Burns this afternoon. The team was eliminated from the tournament after the fourth game; he did not step on the field the entire four games. Pray for me, Harry, as I try to understand the adults we trusted to coach our son; pray that I'll find the strength and wisdom to practice forgiveness. If my current feelings are any indication of the challenge ahead, I'm going to need a lot of prayer.

Much love, my friend,

Janet

JULY 26, 1996

Angelkeep

Dear Harry,

There is a single truth running through the experiences of my life, a reality of living that I hold firmly in mind in order to traverse a sometimes difficult road with my family, and it is this: The act is ours, the consequence God's. Perhaps it seems a stretch to apply this philosophy to baseball disappointments and a slow dying, but I have been trying to understand the fear that leads a human being to believe he must control the consequences, to win at any cost. It must be a fear of not having enough, of not being the best, of living a life that is not written on the pages of history for the next generation; a fear that the consequence of living will simply be death, and so the living must yield measurable results— a trophy, a prize, a fortune renamed.

We do this to prove an evolution beyond animal form, to live fully as human beings, to fight until the end regardless of the cost, and we make great strides for humanity as a result; there is no doubt that human beings have evolved because of this will to measure success. But the consequences are often material—success for the child of man. The wise person is concerned with spiritual consequences—success for the child of God. The rise of the human spirit has nothing to do with winning the game, but with how the game is played. God cares nothing for the trophy or the prize or the fortune renamed, but for the truth, the beauty, and the goodness revealed inning by inning.

And so I am proud of my son, the ballplayer who stood at the fence and cheered for his teammates despite his own great disappointment; the child who shed a few tears, carefully folded his game shirt, and waited for the team picnic with anticipation. I told Michael I am more proud of his strong spirit than his baseball skill, infinitely more proud because good has come from disappointment, and success from the loss of a game. I see these results as a microcosm of eternity, an indication that the evolution from the material to the spiritual is success unto itself.

I have not yet had a response from the Little League board to the letters I wrote, which is curious, since they held a meeting several days ago. At this point, the consequences of raising the issue have less to do with my son than with how the game is played in the years to come. It is also true that spiritual consequences cannot be measured in new rules and regulations, but only within the soul of the individual, and therefore, the consequences do indeed belong to God.

The potential to evolve from the material toward the spiritual—to grow toward God—is invested in every experience, especially the dying process it seems to me, although I'm not the one dying. But if I could convince my mother of this truth, she might find peace.

Michael and I traveled to The Dalles last weekend, and Mother slept the entire time, which leads me to wonder if her dying process has been internalized, if she is preparing herself within the gentle realm of a peaceful slumber; she may have accepted the inevitability of impending death and found her faith in the quiet of a sleeping mind. Perhaps she grows toward God like a miracle, an event unexplained by the laws of nature.

On the active days she sends good-bye letters to family and friends. They are matter-of-fact "I have lost the battle" form letters with a sentence or two of unstable handwriting in the margin. She gives thanks to friends for cards and gifts, says she is not afraid to die, and then asks for one last hug. If I was not so committed to lending strength to Mom, I would have shed tears upon the reading; the courage and desperation with which she faces her fading life burned from those few simple words.

There is still food in the freezer after three months, food that should have been shared long ago. Many of her friends have not come to visit despite their early pledges to do so, and now my mother appeals to them for the final time: Just one more hug, please.

Perhaps it's not the dying woman who needs to hear of acts and consequences, but those who fear her death, who fear the loss of life and love and avoid doing the right thing as a result. How many of us have turned our backs on the dying because of fear? How many of us have realized too late that time does not wait for the timid to find courage, that now is the time to act? Courage is found by facing death head-on, by sharing eternal friendship in the final moments, by standing together regardless of fear. The act is ours, the consequence God's. Oh! how I wish her friends understood. Mom sent seventy letters; maybe her courage will open a heart or two, will challenge a soul to action.

I know a few coaches who could benefit from a lesson in acts and consequences; perhaps my son's courage to cheer at the fence will challenge a soul to evolve beyond winning. Michael handed Mom his game shirt with a proud smile when he walked through the door. Children can be such an inspiration.

Well, Harry, the conference is less than a week away. I am looking forward to meeting your children; perhaps our sons can throw a ball around just for fun!

With much love,

Janet

AUGUST 18, 1996

Angelkeep

Dear Harry,

Even though it feels like high summer, with temperatures in the eighties and nineties, the children return to school in two weeks. Michael will be home schooled, so we are busy collecting books and a computer and plans for the expansion of his young mind. He is eager to face a new challenge, to invest time in learning, to become responsible for the progress of his own life. He talks of international business and red sports cars and the cell phones he will use to make business deals with the moneyed in Japan; he thinks he might export morel mushrooms.

And I talk of training the mind, of unlimited possibilities, of laying the foundation for success. I talk of human struggle and the will to succeed and the fact that his heroes ate peanut butter sandwiches for many years before they were ready to take the business world by storm. I want him to understand that "sudden success" takes years to prepare for. Prepare well, I tell him, and the sky is the limit.

My mother has prepared well for success, it seems. The letters she mailed motivated many of her friends to call, to send cards, and to visit. My role as primary support has been diffused in the social whirlwind that now surrounds her, and I stand back to watch Mom reap a harvest of friendships planted and nurtured over the course of her active life. Details are beyond her confused mind, however; she never seems to know what day it is, or whom she last talked with, or which visitor is knocking on the door. But she seems happy—like a child with a birthday and a dozen adoring friends crowded around.

My sister and her family drove ten hours from California to visit last weekend, so I made a fast trip to the The Dalles and rented a hotel suite with a pool just five feet outside the back door. Mom rallied her strength and joined us for the evening. She sat in her flowered bathrobe and white head covering and faced the pool, content to watch her five grandchildren splash and dunk and squeal with delight. My dad sat outside in a white plastic chair, smoking his cigar and reading the *Nickel* ads. My sister and I folded towels, ran for tea bags, poured soda into paper cups, and generally busied ourselves with the surface demands of family life.

The presence of the dying woman in the middle of the room—the woman with the swollen face and deep bags under fading eyes, the woman with the fleeting mind who brought my sister and me into this world—expanded the parameters of the whole to include both life and death, health and illness, waxing and waning. I beheld the scene with reverence: The full range of human existence moved in and out of that hotel room like respiration—from toddlers to teens to adults to elders—and each person occupied a unique space defined by time; every family member reflected both potential and actual living in the language of flesh and blood. Three generations created the diverse and harmonious music of a shared family life, music that flowed through the little steps and ragged breaths of the ages, music that embraced the whole. My mother smiled and announced she wanted to stay in our hotel room forever. But alas, more friends called to schedule visits, and I returned home with the children.

You may have heard the West is on fire. Half a million acres in Oregon have burned—or are still burning—during the past month. Fine white ash falls from the sky like snow, and the mountains are obscured with a thick and smoky haze. When I drive the road to our cabin, I always wonder if the layer of smoke ribboned across the tops of nearby trees is the result of fire on our side of the mountain, but there are no flames within twenty-five miles; smoke from a distant fire moves across the valley and is captured by the ridge. Every morning the sun rises blood-red and every evening it sets the same way.

Fire and thirst send animals down the mountain, especially coyotes and bears. A neighbor called early this morning and asked if his trapper could set traps on our land. It seems three of his lambs were killed by coyotes, and then a bear dragged a carcass across the road to feast on the remains. We saw a bear yesterday, a six-month-old the size of our Siberian husky romping around near the road. Was this the bear that chewed the lamb the coyotes killed? we wondered. We also wondered where the mother was; the cub seemed too young to survive alone. Keith and the children followed the bear into the forest a hundred yards, but Mom was nowhere to be seen. A blessing if you ask me—a mother bear is a fierce opponent when she thinks her cub is at risk. We had a lively conversation around the dinner table about what will happen to the cub if the mother is dead, and the quick synopsis is that we will not be raising a bear cub; absolutely not.

My mother's illness is progressing as expected. She is heavy and round from the prednisone—a steroid used as an anti-inflammatory—and increasingly hoarse. There is an empty look in her eyes, as if her mind cannot reach beyond the flesh, and her short-term memory seems to have vanished. As long as people are near she is cheerful, but as soon as the door closes her anger rises, raw and irrational. My father is losing a lot of weight, but I have no way of knowing if this is the result of health or more disease. We are all coping as best we can, but I feel a bit out of touch, Harry. I already miss the days when I traveled to keep Mom company, when I massaged her hands and feet and we talked of spiritual things.

There are few days left for intimacy, and now that school is starting, few days left for travel. We enter phase two of Mom's dying process, a time when friends are gathering to say good-bye and my role is diminished somewhat. Phase three will be the end, a time when family draws near and the dying unfolds in force, a time when I'll actively mother my mother again, a time for closure. I am thankful for the phases, for the opportunity to move through the entire dying process with Mom as opposed to the sudden deaths some friends must face when illness unfolds in secret and the end is a shocking and painful surprise.

This is a meaningful time for my family: My son prepares for life while my mother prepares for death, and fires rage on the mountains around us. We transcend the uncertainty with love and faith, and give thanks for every day we have to spend together—for every phone call Mom can still answer and every drive up the mountain to a cabin still standing. Mortal life seems so precarious when viewed as a simple matter of life and death, of having and losing. But we rise to the challenge and find our strength in the reality of the spirit, in the heights of our understanding and the depths of our relationships. We know that neither death nor fire can separate us from the love of God or from each other. Eternity beckons and the soul prepares and for this we live and die.

Hope all is well with you, my friend. It was a pleasure to meet your son at the conference; I was impressed by the gentle way you two relate.

Love,

Janet

Dear Harry,

Merciful ministry defines my mother: Despite her anger, she has always treated others with wisdom and love. She has ministered to the downhearted with words of strength and a fresh berry pie; she has nursed the sick with words of hope and a vase of flowers; she has raised her children with unconditional love and a willingness to meet on equal terms. And now in her final days Mom wants mercy, not pity and fear; she wants hugs, not tears. Her letter to friends was a courageous expression of this need for mercy: "I am not afraid to die, but I need to see you one last time."

There is evidence of false mercy—pity and unwise charity—in my own front yard: The bear cub we saw on the road has now adopted our family and hovers at the back door and on the porch in search of leftovers. A year ago voters approved a confusing referendum that outlawed the use of dogs to hunt bear in the mountains; I was among those who voted for the shadow of mercy in the bear wars. And now the bear population is booming. They feast on elk calves and wander down the mountain in search of food. The elk herd has been decimated, and those living on the edge of the wilderness have hungry bears in the yard.

Our motherless cub raided the garbage and rifled the children's toy kitchen in search of stray Cheerios. We have not seen the mother and worry about the survival of such a small cub. He is six months old, very cute, and equally dangerous—even small cubs can rip through skin with claws designed to climb trees. "Too many bears and not enough traps," Fish and Wildlife told us when we called for help.

Suppression of fire is another false mercy—one that rises from fear. For the past fifty years we have excelled at putting out fires, some of which should have burned unchecked as they have for millions of years. Fire cleans the forest of undergrowth, adds nutrients to the soil, and germinates a variety of dormant seeds. As a result of our aggressive policy to suppress fire, we have tinder-dry forests with a thick and homogeneous undergrowth—fuel for crown fires that race down a mountain and burn so hot, the trees explode. I sleep with the windows wide open and dream of escape.

Mercy is not simply kindness, but a willingness to minister with wisdom and love; mercy is not simply conservation, but a willingness to manage with fire and prevention. Fire enriches the soil like suffering strengthens the soul, proof that mercy will prevail in the fullness of time.

The fullness of time descends upon my mother in the outpouring of love from her family and friends. She has earned these gifts with her unwavering belief in the power of love. Even though fires have raged many times through her life, mercy always seems to rise from the fertile soil of her loving heart.

I enjoyed our conversation last week, Harry. It feels wonderful to get back to the rhythm of life and to watch the seasons change; change is good. Rain would be great.

With fondness and love,

Janet

AUGUST 29, 1996

Angelkeep

Dear Harry,

An oasis of grace has descended upon my mother. The pain in her chest and shoulder has diminished, her memory has returned, and she is awake most of the day. She sounds wonderful on the phone and laughs about the unexplained improvement in her health.

"I'm not even mad at the doctors anymore," she claims.

With all the company she has had, all the prayers, cards, and flowers that have arrived, it is no surprise that she feels better. Mom is even beginning to believe in the power of prayer, which is an evolution for her. She has always assumed that prayer could heal the body, and when the cancer continued to spread, she felt her prayers and the prayers of her friends had been ignored. "God's not even listening!" she cried on many occasions.

I tried to explain that prayer changes the mind of the one who prays; like spiritual exercise, prayer changes the whole by strengthening each part.

"Even though your material body does not heal, Mom, every prayer uplifts the spirit of the one who prays, and the one for whom the prayer is offered."

She is beginning to understand. Many of those who pray for Mom have recently come to give her a hug, and the personal contact brings the prayer to life; she feels better because those who pray for her are standing near. There is no better medicine than the touch of two hands and two hearts and two minds praying for courage and strength, for peace and love, for a merciful end to a long suffering.

A rainstorm moved through the area yesterday, bringing heavy showers to our parched mountains. The air has been cleaned of smoke, the undergrowth has been partially watered, and the fires raging around us have been mostly contained. The fire season will officially end when the first snow falls in mid-October, but the rains have brought a reprieve, and I slept soundly last night for the first time in several weeks, waking with renewed appreciation for the beauty and diversity of life on the edge of the wilderness.

When I drive toward the mountain along wheat fields and farms, it is common to startle a covey of quail moving from one side of the dirt road to the other. They turn in unison, like a spontaneous wave, and retreat to the dry grass that grows four feet tall along the road, golden stalks that shimmer in sunlight and sway with incredible grace; golden stalks that call to the outstretched hand, "Run your palm along our crowns of ripe summer grain." Into the grass runs the mother quail with up to a dozen little chicks trailing behind, and I am reminded of the children's book entitled *Madeline* and a line that ends, "with twelve little girls in two straight lines."

The roads become like washboards this time of year when heavy threshing machines are moved from field to field, leaving behind deep impressions in the thick dust and occasional mud. The valley is quilted with squares of golden wheat and green grass, and dotted with bales of hay and herds of buffalo that feast on the remnants of the harvest. The deer roam just above the tree line, finding sweet wildflowers everywhere they turn. We saw a pair of five-point bucks lounging on a hill by the side of the road. Fearless and peaceful, they watched us pass without running away; they seemed to know by instinct that we carried neither bow nor gun.

And so the grace of nature fills these summer days, an oasis before the transition of fall and the harshness of winter on the mountain. My mother seems filled with the spirit of the summer season, and the love of friends. And I am filled with the rhythm of mountain life—with the ebb and flow of fire and rain, with the calm before the storm.

Hope all is well with you, my friend. Talk with you soon.

With love,

Janet

EPTEMBER 3, 1996

Angelkeep

Dear Harry,

I don't know where I heard the line "Wait a week and everything will change," but the person who quipped such a truism must have had a mother dying, a few kids to raise, and a stormy relationship with mountain weather. I generally like change, but these days change is not self-directed; change descends without warning, and sometimes without mercy.

I find myself becoming increasingly resistant to Mom's mood swings—irritated by her tendency to globalize trifles and indulge in self-pity, distant and filled with disdain for the time she spends riding the violent winds of her own creation, saddened by how familiar these feelings seem. There must have been times in my

And so now you know, Harry. I'm not ashamed of being human and realize these feelings are fairly normal. I'll feel better tomorrow—in fact, I'm feeling better already. And when I talk to my mother, I'll encourage her to vent because I know that even the slightest resistance on my part would fuel the fire. My other side must be satisfied by a purging with words on paper, an acknowledgment that I have another side, a healthy and quiet release between friends.

Storms battered the mountain last night. Rain descended in waves and woke me from sleep a dozen times; like handfuls of rice upon our blue steel roof, the rain fell with force and then suddenly stopped—fell again and stopped. In the silence, new storms quickly moved into position above our heads and burst into being with bright flash and quick boom; lightning and thunder surrounded the cabin.

This morning we woke to sunshine and a heavy layer of fresh snow on the ridge. The cabin was unusually cold—below sixty degrees—and the garden was threatened by frost. A thin layer of woodsmoke hovered above the village as I drove deserted roads to my daughter's school. The only truck we passed was filled with rounds of firewood; a bearded driver offered a friendly wave. Our world was fresh with the promise of a new season: with turning leaves and cold winds and woodsmoke that speaks of warm hearts gathered around the hearth. The fear of summer wildfires will soon fade into memory, and gratitude for the harvest will rise from the ashes. In all things, the promise of another harvest sustains us.

Well, my friend, life and death march on, and I learn another truth: Nature cannot be denied—tempered and tamed perhaps, but never denied; especially human nature. Challenges arise without our consent, and we respond as best we can—sometimes with mercy, but more often with anger and frustration. After all, mercy is an evolutionary process, a rich and beautiful harvest that requires a long growing season. My mother and I are both still growing, and I know you are as well. Despite all the trials, I feel truly grateful because I want above all to grow—to become mercy personified just like the Master.

Take care, Harry.

With fondness and love,

Janet

S EPTEMBER 9, 1996

Angelkeep

Dear Harry,

The air surrounding our cabin is filled with the sweet smell of fir pitch and the sound of dueling chain saws. Michael works beside his father with his own, smaller cutting machine; power tools have become a rite of passage for this male child. They harvest the dead timber from the surrounding forest, de-limbing logs and dragging them next to the cabin with a 1950 John Deere tractor we call Poppin' John because of the pop! pop! pop! sound and puffs of smoke that emerge from the exhaust chimney on top of the hood. Our old friend has a new coat of green paint and a classic persona that delights the young visitors who always beg for a tractor ride. Keith—in overalls and hard hat—will lift one, two, or sometimes even three small children onto his lap and take a slow and noisy crawl around the logging roads. Better than a horse, if you ask me.

The entire family gathers firewood during the month of September. Rachel and Hannah each wear a small pair of leather gloves to protect their tiny hands from slivers and pitch. After the boys cut the logs into rounds, the girls roll them to the pile, creating a mountain of eighteen-inch sections that will be split and stacked before winter sets in. We heat our small cabin with wood, burning four or five cords every year.

After an hour or two, the girls become restless with repetition and invariably begin building relationships between whatever objects of similar size they can find within an easy reach. Little Hannah solves crisis after crisis with her pine cone family, rescuing dozens of screaming children who are pushed over the edge of the stump house by the resident bully. On the next stump over, Rachel negotiates marriages between various branches of the family tree; brothers and sisters and cousins marry with abandon.

And someone always seems to be dying, an event that involves the entire community. It begins with Rachel's whispered announcement: "I think she's dying." And then according to script Hannah moves in with a handful of relatives, solemnly bows her head, and waits for instructions.

"She's very sick. Keep the children quiet," Rachel continues after carefully placing one of the largest pine cones in the center of the stump. Hannah picks up the remaining pine cones one at a time and shushes them, frowning seriously.

The girls cover the unfortunate cone with piles of torn leaves to keep her warm, and decide to take the rest of the family for a swim in the watering can. After they move the entire collection of cones and branches to the swimming place, they send the mother back to the stump every three minutes or so until Hannah suddenly announces, "She's dead." The girls look at each other in silence for a few awkward seconds while they wonder what to do next, and then quickly agree to abandon the family in favor of the clubhouse and rope swing.

I marvel at the way my children play, practicing their relationships and preparing for trauma one make-believe step at a time. Tomorrow they will likely revisit the scene in order to search for a less awkward end. But they still won't know what to do with the cone because they have no experience with death and burial. They could decide on a miracle cure, but then the game would feel surreal. They know Grandmother's death is inevitable, and they face it head-on in their own unique way.

Lessons of life and death abound in the forest. Whenever Keith and I go for a walk, we look for damaged or dead trees to cut for firewood. We are novices in the field of silvaculture and so always wonder what pestilence or disease turns green needles to rust, what natural forces squeeze the life from a struggling tree. The most familiar blight, mistletoe, causes dwarfed limbs to grow in dense clumps around an otherwise healthy trunk that is soon strangled to death. Some trees—giant ones that fall to the ground in wet or windy weather—suffer the effects of old age, but others— offspring in their prime—are victims of disease and stand ragged and rusting amid an otherwise healthy grove of trees.

I think of the forest as a family of trees in various stages of life, with size and color an indication of age and health. I wonder which tree has spawned the seedlings that grow in the soft loam on the forest floor, and which young sapling will survive long enough to shade my children's grandchildren, and which currently healthy mother will succumb to disease before her time.

I was sorry to hear about the flood at your farm. Hurricanes seem such exotic storms to this Northwest native, but I know the results can be devastating. Mother nature negotiates neither disease nor weather with mortals, unfortunately.

Anyway, thanks for your letter, Harry. The timing for your encouragement was perfect, as usual.

Love,

Janet

SEPTEMBER 21, 1996

Angelkeep

Dear Harry,

My mind is filled with misty scenes and wild sensations from my week on the Oregon coast. Three long years have passed since I last gazed upon the Pacific, and my hunger was almost palpable.

Once there I realized why: Every part of the rugged sea-coast formed a piece of my childhood puzzle, a puzzle that stretched two hundred miles from Seaside to Florence, a puzzle awaiting the gentle tap of inquiring mind to bind memories one with another. Together these memories transformed my hunger into a familiar sense of place, a meaning assigned to land and sea beyond the natural beauty: In this little town we were happy as a family; on that long beach my young mother sunned herself while we dug the sand with oyster shells and attacked each other with seaweed swords.

I remembered the white sacks of saltwater taffy purchased for fifty cents at a sidewalk counter still open for business after thirty years. I remembered the magic of driftwood bonfires and chocolate s'mores as I walked past charred piles still smoldering after a night on the beach. I remembered endless days exploring ocean caves and walking alone to the weathered little store on Highway 101, a childhood landmark completely surrounded by new condos and golf courses. I remembered a thousand pleasures that are now part of the whole and realized why my heart flutters and my lungs fill with every view of the magnificent Pacific: The ocean is filled with memories that wash upon the shore of my mind in gentle waves—remember this . . . remember that . . . remember me.

We traveled south along the coastline for two days, stopping at roadside attractions to study seals and whales, braving wind and rain at ocean viewpoints to watch black-suited surfers ride the changing tide.

I bought an angel pin for Mom at Cape Foulweather, named by Captain Cook following five days of intense winds that will forever plague the cape. Captain Cook braved the winds to chart the coastline, literally putting Oregon on the map in 1778.

During the middle of the week I called my parents and stumbled upon a horrendous fight. The details are without merit, but the sound of crashing pots and screaming voices will linger long after my mother's demise. I was speechless and battered by the intensity of the exchange I was witnessing over the phone line. After spending several days remembering the joys of childhood on the beach, it was unnerving to suddenly find myself in the middle of such a traumatic event.

Within minutes of ending the call, the motel room felt stuffy and cramped, so Keith and I ordered pizza for the children and quickly escaped to find the nearest pool table. My husband listened patiently while I complained about the irrational behavior of my beloved mother.

"Why can't she just grow up," I said, and then hit the cue ball entirely too hard with my pool stick. Keith shrugged and smiled faintly. After a while I calmed down and tried to define the situation in a more rational manner.

"She's not going to change, and I'm not going to abandon her," I said with a heavy sigh, feeling frustrated and defiant at the same time. "But I'm really tired of these emotional outbursts."

"Just try to let it go, Janet," Keith said, and sank the eight ball to win the game. "She is who she is."

Without fail, playing pool challenges me to shift my focus from the part to the whole. I gain a unique philosophic perspective from the physics of the game: The system of angles and relationships, the required finesse, force, luck, and skill, become a microcosm of life, a metaphor for the successes and failures of living in material form. I can line everything up just right, focus my will, utilize all my skill, and the ball still bounces off the rail. The physics of the game are perfect, but alas, my mastery of physics is not. Keith beat me four games out of four, but I discovered a solution while searching in vain for the perfect angle and it was this: Life is a struggle.

I know it sounds simpleminded, Harry, but I found relief in this vision of life as one all-encompassing struggle, a concept quite distinct from suffering. I realized that struggle is the inevitable tension between the individual and the environment, while suffering is just one possible result. Without struggle there would be no opportunity for either suffering or success, and no hope for progress.

After expanding my view to embrace the whole, I found enough strength to diffuse my emotional response to our family trauma. Since life is a struggle, why worry about a few banging pots? I decided. But I called my parents three times before deciding to visit on the way home.

My mother laughed when I gave her the angel pin purchased at Cape Foulweather. "I wish I'd had this two days ago," she said with a sheepish smile. Our radiator hose burst in the driveway, a sure sign that our decision to stop in The Dalles was the right one. After a three-hour delay for repairs, we headed home.

And now, Harry, I must make another honest confession. During my brief visit with Mom I was simply going through the motions: the kisses, the small favors, the small talk. Instead of her slipping away, I was pulling away—standing at arm's length even while my arms were firmly wrapped around her; a fear-based defense against pain, an attempt to escape the struggle.

Or perhaps I was just numb—it's unusual for me to seek comfort in emotional distance. During forty years of living I have learned that progress is rarely made by those who seek comfort. Progress is made by those who push beyond comfort, through the struggle, into the world beyond. Progress is made by those who go the eleventh mile even though they were exhausted by the first ten. Am I such a person? Can I reconnect with Mom despite the risk of trauma and tears? Can I move beyond my own resistance, beyond the self-defense that pleads enough is enough?

Captain Cook stayed five days to chart the coastline even though he was physically battered by relentless winds. My parents enjoyed our three-hour visit even though they were emotionally battered by angry waves. How can they suffer so much and still smile? I wonder. "Because we forgive each other," I hear my mother quietly say. Because forgiveness melts every resistance like a rising sun upon the morning frost.

I will shine the light of forgiveness upon my own life and watch the ice turn to sea. And I will learn to ride the changing tides.

I pray all is well with you, my friend, and that the changing tides in your life take you where you hope to go.

With loving regards,

Janet

Fall

SEPTEMBER 23, 1996

Angelkeep

Dear Harry,

As a first step in my eleventh mile with Mom I decided
to really listen to her angry outbursts, to lower my own defenses
in order to feel the depth of her frustration and pain. She was at
the end of her rope, she said, and finally decided not to expect
understanding from her family and friends. She was using anger
to get her way because no one was listening to her appeals and
pleadings; no one understood her loneliness.

"My friends talk of vacations and new condos," Mom
sobbed. "I ask a few questions to be polite, but we have nothing
in common anymore; my life is meaningless. Meaningless!" Her
incredible sobs reached across the phone line and finally shook
me awake.

I wanted to say, "Mom, you've lived a great, meaningful
life," but she beat me to it.

"People give me all kinds of advice—what to feel, what
to be thankful for—but they don't know what it's like to be
dying," she yelled into the phone. "I just want to live while I'm
able, to have some fun, but no one understands."

Over the months (years, actually) I've learned that all the standard responses make Mom more angry, and so I don't ask her what she wants to do, and I don't remind her of all the offers for lunches or movies or country drives she's had—activities the rest of us consider fun. She wants exceptional excitement; she wants to put normal life behind her and enter a fantasy world where she can forget the cancer growing across her chest and through her lungs; she wants to gamble, I realized all of a sudden.

"Let's take a trip to Wildhorse Casino, Mom, just the two of us," I say to her. "I'll come and get you Friday night."

Silence—incredible silence and then a deep breath. "Really?" she says quietly. I work out the details one sentence at a time, and while we're planning this spontaneous trip over the phone, I come to understand that it is exactly the right thing to do: I need time alone with her, she needs a gambling companion, and my dad needs a couple of days all to himself.

He was thrilled. "I'll put her pills in little boxes, Janet. You will do just fine," he said with great relief when I asked him if I could steal her for the weekend.

And so the two of us are going gambling, Harry. I'll follow her around with a little bucket and chase nickels across the carpet just like old times. It will be six months to the day since we left Las Vegas, six months of hard living with my dying mother. It's time for a little fun and I can hardly wait.

Much love,

Janet

Dear Harry,

All aspects of life are motivated by hunger, I've decided: physical life by the need to nourish the body; emotional life by the need to nourish the character; spiritual life by the need to nourish the soul. We are hungry by design and basically become what our appetites lead us to consume.

The hunger at Wildhorse Casino was as thick as blinding fog on a still morning, as thick as the smoke from a thousand cigarettes; more than half the gamblers smoke with abandon, it seems. The hunger pulsed like Times Square at midnight, hummed like a freeway moving beyond rush hour, buzzed like a Singapore marketplace on a Saturday morning; the hunger seemed to lift the body up and carry it from machine to machine with colorful seduction—Play Three! Win 10,000! Wild! Hot! Fun!—and every once in a while the hunger was punctuated by the cries of a winner.

Heads at nearby machines would briefly turn and then return to the task at hand: inserting bills, pushing buttons, watching the spin of images on a screen, exhaling, inhaling, pushing, pushing, pushing.

I was a little disappointed, Harry, because they don't use coins at the new casinos; the sound of dimes, quarters, and dollars plunking into metal bins is dying a slow death. No more chasing runaway coins across the carpet either. My job consisted of taking little printed tickets to the cashier and exchanging them for more bills. I soon learned to ask for ones and fives instead of twenties— big bills are too easily spent by fast fingers on a flashing button.

Winners receive the satisfying sound of quick tones that start low and move high, similar to the sound of a container filling on Saturday morning cartoons. The more you win, the more tones you receive—along with credits—and when you win big, like a few lucky souls happened to do, the tones move from low to high in rapid succession like a police siren; those who hear the sound know that something serious has happened nearby.

Although my mother was pale and slow, she seemed to fit right in. At first I was worried the staff might think I had kidnapped her from a hospital and was planning foul play—she was so weak and sick, she slept in the backseat of the Lincoln the entire trip to the casino and then woke with wig and clothes askew. Because our room was not yet ready, Mom struggled to paint her face and comb her wig in the car. We finally decided not to care how she looked;

she was dying after all. We both felt a sense of satisfaction from facing this truth, as if we moved in a world all our own and suspended the rules at will.

The minute we walked into the casino, she started playing dollar machines by the door but soon realized the three hundred she had to gamble with would fly through her fingers in no time at all, so we moved to the bank of quarter machines nearby. After three hours pushing buttons we decided to feed our bodies instead, but Mom felt too sick to eat—it was all I could do to get her back to the room.

Both her weakness and her loss of appetite were pronounced during the two days we spent together: She would hold the mascara brush to her eye and become winded; she would eat a bite or two and become full. I dispensed medication every four hours and tended to her bleeding chest morning and night, cleaning the deep caverns of leathery flesh with cotton balls and peroxide, and applying a salve with my gloved finger. We rested two hours and then went for round two at the casino.

The reason she fit right in was that many of the gamblers were also silver-haired retired types—the parking lot was filled with motor homes. The desert casino was built on Indian land one mile from the freeway and surrounded by acres of dust and grain—not an exit to take without cause. The majority of gamblers fit into three categories: retired travelers, truckers, and locals. Because the casino was dry—the Walla Walla tribes do not permit alcohol anywhere on the reservation—the only reason to venture through the doors was to gamble. The retired majority were spending excess funds for entertainment; the truckers were seeking relief from the road and possibly a new career; the locals of every race and age seemed intent on winning—an addiction created from uncontrolled hunger, I believe.

Sunday morning we woke from a deep sleep around eight o'clock. Mom was so weak, she could not stand by herself from a prone position in the bath. "If not for you," she told me later, "I would not have left the bed." We spent two hours getting ready and then made our way to the casino for the third and final round. She sat at the same nickel machine for three hours, spending less than twenty dollars and finding satisfaction from quietly playing the game. When we left the casino a few hours later, there were several large bills still stuffed in her little blue purse.

I'll never drive by exit 216 again without thinking of our weekend together. In the hotel room we lay on double beds and held long conversations about anger and death, about children and grandchildren. I asked if she was afraid of dying, and she said, "No, honey, I'm not afraid. I know where I'm going." But she looked at me with tears in her eyes and said, "I am afraid of the pain. I want the pain to stop."

Then she offered advice regarding the children. She told

me to go easy on Michael, to focus less on his shortcomings and more on his strengths. "He's a good boy," she said, just like a grandmother. "Loving and kind."

And she made me promise to find piano lessons for Rachel. "She's such a smart girl. I'm sure she'll become more confident if she learns to play music."

"I'm still grateful for my own lessons, Mom." I said.

"See," she said, and smiled. "Mothers do know some things."

Mom thought of Hannah and teared up again. "She won't even remember me," she said. "She's too young." She told me not to hurry Hannah, to enjoy her while she was still little. "She'll grow up fast, Janet. You won't believe how fast."

Before she drifted to sleep, we talked about her final days. Without any prompting she promised to control her anger, and then asked if I would visit more often because for some reason I don't upset her. "It's always been that way, Mom," I said to her, and she smiled.

Needless to say, Harry, my resistance has been replaced once again by a desire to mother my mother, to soothe her aches and pains. There were several times during our weekend when she spoke irrationally, completely unaware of the intensity of her emotions, but I said nothing. Her emotional hunger will be resolved soon enough, and then anger will never again rise within my mother's heart.

Thanks for your call last week, Harry. It was nice to hear your voice.

With loving regards,

Janet

OCTOBER 7, 1996

Angelkeep

Dear Harry,

From a distance I can see that the tamaracks have finally started to turn yellow just below the ridge, a true yardstick by which to measure the progress of the changing seasons. These tall deciduous trees are scattered among the evergreens and invisible from the road until their fall colors emerge. Old-timers say the snow will set in when the needles of the tamarack cover the ground, but first the branches will slowly turn from green to orange, forming bright ribbons across the bodice of the mountainside, and the peaks above will dress in a thin veil of virgin white. And then the needles will fall in a final dance with the winter wind, the light upon bare branches will dim, the forest floor will be covered in a soft blanket of fresh snow, and the tamaracks will sleep for another season.

But it's hard to imagine the brisk fall and cold winter just ahead while Indian summer illuminates the maple trees with brilliant light. I bathe my eyes in the translucent beauty of a thousand red suns shimmering in a warm wind. Summer has been captured and held by high pressure even though we are a month beyond the first frost—an official Indian summer—and the weather is dazzling.

Last Friday I sat on the cabin steps in the sun and talked with Mom about how God could allow her to suffer so much.

"How does my suffering contribute anything to the heavenly worlds?" she wanted to know over the phone. "And if God is so merciful, why doesn't he do something?" she cried with the intensity only those in pain can muster—raw, heartfelt pleadings that drove me to the pickup and down the freeway a few hours later.

Mom and I have diverse theologies regarding pain and suffering, as you know. She believes that suffering is punishment for some wrongdoing, and relief by one's own hand would be another sin. I believe suffering is a fact of mortal existence and that God encourages the practice of mercy in whatever form our faith allows. She knows not to replace a lifetime of religious belief with a consolation; she prays for enough strength to make it to Dad's seventieth birthday on October 25th, and then for a quick, natural death.

That night when I sat by her bed, she thanked me for coming: "When you're here, Janet, I feel human. Otherwise I'm like

Dr. Jekyll and Mr. Hyde." Her eyes teared up and she cried, "My friends call me an inspiration, but they don't know what I'm like with your father. I'm so sorry for how I treat him; the most horrible things fall from my mouth. It's like poison."

I held her hand, stroked her arm, and listened quietly while the truth fell from her chapped lips without hesitation, as if all barriers to self-awareness had finally been destroyed by pain. I saw anger turn to grief, a transformation rare and moving. "It hurts so much when my friends leave because I may never see them again," she cried with pain-filled eyes. And then without a moment's warning I saw grief turn to anger when Dad walked through the room; he has become her target.

I counseled Dad to build a shield around himself, a double-thick shield to protect him from her anger, but he knows these things already. He surprised me with his comment that life is meaningful because he is helping someone else, and that he plans to volunteer at the senior center after Mom is gone.

I'm still trying to understand the man my father has become: He is an enigma—without religious convictions but filled with spiritual truth—the result of forty-four years living with and caring for my loving and irrational mother. He praises her, citing the dozens of friends who have brought meals, sent cards, and visited recently.

"She has thrown her bread upon the water," he said, and it

is true—my mother has always been the first on a friend's doorstep with a casserole. It is also true that my father has been transformed through suffering; there is no other way to make sense of his desire to care for the sick and downhearted but to assume he has discovered truth through service.

I have worried for him unnecessarily, which is a common reality of the human experience: We tend to harbor anxiety. But as the saying goes, "The disappointments hardest to bear are those which never come." Even though his health is failing, he seems strong—smiling through tired eyes, searching through cupboards for an unused pasta machine he wants me to have, ignoring Mom's countless digs and outbursts.

The friendships my parents have cultivated over the years astound me. The quality of the people who care for them is a testimony to the life they have lived, a testimony to the volume and quality of bread they both have scattered upon the water.

The phone rang every twenty minutes on Sunday, and I was impressed by the sincere exchange of endearments between my mother and the friends on the other end of the line. She called them "honey" and "dear" regardless of age or relationship, as if the dying process has conferred upon her the title of elder. And she sounded peaceful, unfazed by the blood oozing from open sores or the wheezing from lungs surely invaded by dangerous fluids. She was an inspiration, and I experienced another sudden understanding that much of the strength my father and I share has come from this side of my mother—from the woman who gently counsels others even in the midst of her own great suffering.

The drive home along the Columbia was beautiful. The occasional colors of the changing season were reflected by the calm surface of the river, a perfect mirror. My beloved river has been in the news again because of the discovery of a 9,300-year-old skeleton along the riverbank near Walla Walla last summer. The local tribes have claimed the remains as an ancestor and are trying to end all plans the archaeologists have for research, saying it would be a desecration. Lawyers are filing suits and countersuits.

What has been learned from simple observation is that the young man died when a spear wound in the hip caused an infection that spread to his brain. I wonder how long the man suffered, and which members of his family sat by his bedside while he withered and died. Or perhaps he died alone, unable to make it home after the trauma that eventually poisoned his entire body. My mother will most likely die from a bacterial infection like many of her ancestors; the pneumonia invading her weak lungs cannot be purged because her lungs have been damaged beyond repair by cancer.

There were many small boats clustered around the mouth of the tributaries that feed into the mighty Columbia; calm water is a clarion call for local fishermen with questionable boats. While looking out the car window at the velvet hills, the timeless men in ancient crafts, the peaceful river on a warm October day, I could not help thinking of the toxins moving with a strong current below the surface.

And I thought of my mother: a woman with her own poisons leaching into mind, poisons caused by a trauma long ago, poisons only partially contained by the strength of her loving heart. Maybe someday humanity will learn to counteract the spread of poisons resulting from trauma, physical and emotional; maybe someday we will discover a miraculous cure for what ails both body and mind; maybe my father already has.

Mom needs the companionship of women now, so my sister and I will take turns staying with her. My father is grateful, and commented that I will be grateful later in life. "I know," I said to him before I left. "I give as much as I can now so I'll never look back and wish I had."

I think of you often, my friend. Hope all is well with you and your family. My sister will cover for me next week, so if Mom's health holds, I'll be able to attend our quarterly meeting in Chicago.

With love,

Janet

O CTOBER 14, 1996

Angelkeep

Dear Harry,

Mother sleeps round the clock, waking when the phone rings, wondering what hour and day it is, speaking in remnants of memories that I strive to trace so we can hold something in common. It is all we have over the wire, these small confused sound bites of fleeting thoughts that seem to hang between us, going nowhere.

"You know that show," she says with effort. "There was something different; it wasn't the same."

The spectrum of language available to her sedated mind is increasingly limited, and I offer options, asking twenty questions with the same matter-of-fact tone I use with my three-year-old who uses the "d" sound to start every new word. As long as I'm patient, Hannah will repeat herself until I understand, but impatience defeats us both on occasion—she gives up and tends to her own needs as best she can.

I capture every half-formed clue Mother offers and synthesize understanding by letting my mind roam through our history at will. "A show?" I ask, and then realize a movie we saw together must have been edited for television, a program she watched last night while lying alone in her water bed. I pretend to remember the movie, pretend to reach the part of mind she has lost.

"They took out all the racy stuff, Mom," I said, and she agreed. "I thought that was it." We struggled to find common ground while sailing through a crippling fog; we settled on a mirage.

For some reason I felt the need to cook a turkey dinner Sunday, rising early to rinse and stuff the bird, becoming the incarnation of my mother in the kitchen. Her presence rose from the onions sautéing in the butter, from the bread crumbs baking in a warm oven; she was the master of turkey dinners. As I wrestled to tuck wings and skewer skin at both ends, I remembered it was she who taught me how. She was standing behind me, giving instructions in full sentences, more fully present in memory than in mirage.

When I told her of my industrious undertaking, she said, "And you're bringing this dinner to me?" I laughed but she was not making a joke, nor was she serious. Like a child who dreams the impossible, she dreams of me standing at her bedside with a steaming plate of roasted turkey; her longing for my presence radiated from every thick word. And I long to be with her, Harry, but I can't leave my three children to fend for themselves while Keith works ten-hour days. I will hire a nanny when the time comes, but I'm not sure when that will be. Do I go now, while she still has the strength of mind to know I'm there, or later, when my father needs me most?

Uncertainty has captured my life and stands guard over every decision; uncertainty has become my constant companion, like a formless shadow that consumes all hope and conceals every dream but one: Beyond Mom's death freedom waits, the freedom to grieve and go on with my life. But the pain of uncertainty pales in the light of a passionate life, I've discovered; a passionate life is my best defense against the all-consuming shadow of Mother's demise.

During the past months my preoccupation with dying has dulled my passion for living, a defense conceived in the mind and born on the screen in front of me. I have lived in the mind, transforming emotion into words and words into philosophy as a way to control my pain and guard my strength. But emotion does not evaporate under the light of a strong mind—emotion needs a drain field, a way to slowly seep into the soil of a human life.

And so I've poked holes in my concept of strength, tried to embrace all of my self, allowed my animal urges and emotional hunger to flow uninhibited, and I've rediscovered my passion. Passion relieves my troubled heart, enhances my sense of self, reconnects me with the living. Passion is the sword I use to battle the shadow of death, to banish the guilt of living well while my mother dies, to defend myself from an invading gloom.

I experienced a personal revelation regarding passion while

playing pool with Keith in the local tavern. While losing my third game I was lamenting the demands of my life—the lack of an office, the little time I have to write, the physical appetites, diseases, and distractions of living in material form.

"I want to evolve beyond the animal, to live more fully as a spiritual being, to focus my mind on the higher realities," I said while lining up an impossible shot. "So do I," Keith said, "but I also want to experience my life as an animal to the fullest extent possible. After all, this is my only chance." And he smiled one of those smiles I've been avoiding, the distracting kind.

Keith has been my silent support, becoming the home parent without question whenever I felt the need to travel, listening without interruption whenever I felt the need to vent. He has nurtured me in various ways while his own needs have been largely ignored. During these seven months of caring for Mom I have rarely asked how he feels about his mother-in-law's slow death. I tell myself this is the benefit of partnership, that our gifts to each other will balance out in the fullness of time, but perhaps I've been self-absorbed at the expense of my husband and children.

As the pool game proceeded, I began to wonder if I've pulled up roots in order to sprout wings—denied my original nature while indulging an active mind. At what cost? I wondered. I visualized planting my feet firmly in the soil of human experience, to feel the pain, the weakness, the fear of being just another Jane with a dying mother losing a pool game in the local tavern, and I looked around at all the other Janes and Joes, the hungry, the happy, the emerging spiritual beings in physical form. And I began to relax, to feel joy, to embrace my dual nature and give thanks that my life had not slipped away while I contemplated eternity, to embrace my passion as a mother and a wife.

I'm feeling stronger, Harry, as if the uncertainty of Mom's death can now coexist with my own demanding life. I have given myself permission to fully live while she slowly dies. In the deep recesses of her fading mind, I know Mom would want it that way.

The weather is changing. A Pacific storm brought wind, rain, and cold air to the mountain last night, and the tamarack needles have started to fall; snow will not be far behind. Can't wait to fly down the mountain with boards strapped to my feet just for fun.

I'll see you soon, my friend.

With love,

Janet

CTOBER 21, 1996

Angelkeep

Dear Harry,

Cold and snow have descended upon us without warning ten days before Halloween, which is our usual benchmark for early winter. Icicles hang from the eves, a thin blanket of crusty snow squeaks underfoot, and clear blue skies belie the fact that the mercury has dropped forty degrees in the past week.

I have been wondering about the motherless bear cub who disappeared a month ago for some mysterious reason; he was surely not driven away by my broom. More likely he was the target of some rifle or bow, an easy target for a rogue hunter who set his sights on the cub one day while preparing his weapon for the upcoming season. Or perhaps the cub fell to a cougar, or a pack of coyotes working as an efficient team, or by some great miracle is curling up in a den about now.

Next spring we'll know for sure because his first step to break the fast will be toward our front porch—a testimony to the ability of the bear to remember the hand that unintentionally feeds him. If he survives the winter, we'll need a larger broom during our next round of negotiations over the garbage; with children in the home we refuse to keep guns where they might be of some use.

However, I was wishing for a firearm a while back to scare away cows that were trimming the grass above the septic tank. The lost herd arrived unannounced one morning and stayed a week before we located the ranchers who were grazing them on open range land fifteen miles west of us. After watching these almost mindless creatures trample streams, eat flowers, and deposit large cow pies around the yard, the guilt I have harbored for falling off the vegetarian bandwagon a few years ago quickly turned to dust.

Keith hit a doe last week while driving home from work. Her unlucky neck was broken when the rest of her body took a sudden right turn around the driver's side of the pickup, causing trauma to both husband and truck. Keith felt sad for killing the deer, although not overly sentimental. He moved the doe to the side of the road and arrived home a little shaken, but hungry for supper nonetheless.

A pond frog with an extra leg was found nearby. An isolated case would raise no alarm, but deformed frogs also have been discovered in Minnesota, South Dakota, Wisconsin, Quebec, Vermont, and now, of course, in my neighborhood pond. Because frogs are accurate bellwethers of biological development—as go the frogs, so go the people—there is great cause for concern.

One theory regarding the widespread deformity is that airborne pollutants descend upon mountains and wetlands, and then collect in ponds and swamps, which are, of course, the primary habitat of frogs. Since mountain streams are the headwaters of the mighty rivers, and wetlands are the surface sponge for the underground water tables, airborne pollution has the potential to damage the entire global environment—frogs first, it seems.

My sister has been in The Dalles a week now, and quivers on the edge between acceptance and angst. I can hear the struggle in her voice, the need to vent her sadness and fear tempered moment by moment with the desire to show her strength and love, hence the unsteady voice. Mom's health is changing for the worse: She is unbalanced when upright, unable to breathe, and too weak to argue—almost. Dad is negotiating with her to accept oxygen and a hospital bed, but Mom refuses to consider the bed; it is the visible symbol of death to her, the end of the fight.

My father's seventieth birthday celebration is Friday, so I will drive to The Dalles with the children on Thursday. Keith will arrive on Saturday for an early Thanksgiving dinner complete with all the trimmings, a promise to Mom. I've been practicing, as you know. This will be the last time we all gather for a family feast, and even my brother is planning to come.

By unspoken agreement, the clan gathers for a death watch. Mom sounds cheerful and distant on the phone, answering questions with a disconnected word or two, unconcerned about the state of her health, it seems. She appears to be fading away while wearing the beautiful demeanor we have all come to love; she drifts upon an inward sea, reaching for loved ones through a changing fog, lucid in waves. At least this is how she sounds from a distance. I have hired a nanny to care for the children, and will stay with Mom for a week or two, or until the end if I can.

The motherless cub, the wandering herd, the unlucky doe, the deformed frog, and my dying mother have all been challenged by unfortunate circumstances and the limits of their material form, but only Mother has a consciousness of free will and a desire to know God; only she will live again in another, more perfect form. Her animal body no longer serves her, and the divine elements of her true self—personality, mind, and soul—prepare for transport beyond this world, beyond the limitations of flesh and blood.

The only way to continue living is to suffer death—to shed the animal form. If I can keep the reality of this transformation firmly in mind and think of her as an emerging spiritual being during the inevitable molting season, the emotional trauma of watching her die might be transformed as well.

I've never done this before, Harry, so I can only hope that my strength remains while Mom drifts away, that I can hold both the animal and the spiritual in the loving embrace of my human heart while the woman who gave me birth approaches her own rebirth. A worthy goal, a challenging task, a learning experience more profound than all others: As her death unfolds, the meaning of life will be fully revealed. Strength ... I pray for strength. And I pray that my faith will temper my grief. Uncertainty leads me into the shadow of my mother's death, but I fear not.

> With love and gratitude for your
> unwavering friendship,
> Janet

NOVEMBER 1, 1996

The Dalles

Dear Harry,

I believe that in the beginning, before time and space, the I AM longed for relationship with the other and creation began. First the Son and the Spirit and the Isle of Paradise—in waves creation extended outward from the Eternal and the Infinite, unfolding potential with matter and mind, stirring a whirlwind of existence with energy and force, endowing even those who crawled from the primordial soup on an evolving world with a spark of God, a unique personality, and a free will.

The Creator could have unfolded perfection, could have filled the infinite universe with eternal beings of love and light who longed only for relationship with the I AM, but there is no adventure in uniformity, no growth in the absolute; the Creator desired that love be returned to the source willingly, without condition or pressure. And so human will is considered sacred throughout the universe of universes; human will is a force allowed to motivate matters of life and death on the worlds of time and space. When my mother willed the timing of her death, this truth became self-evident. Here is the story:

I arrived in The Dalles with the children on Friday morning, October 25th—my father's seventieth birthday. Mom greeted us with a weak smile and a clouded mind, but was filled with gratitude for the flowers we brought her; Rachel and Hannah each offered a rose, and Michael held a beautiful arrangement purchased with money he earned from baby-sitting his sisters.

She lay in her new hospital bed, sleeping and greeting the five grandchildren who wandered in throughout the day, swallowing pills and shuffling to the bathroom between two sets of strong arms, eating a bite or two now and then; her face was pale and swollen. A festive mood prevailed nonetheless.

The oldest children decorated the house for Halloween at Mom's request, and I made meat loaf for Dad's birthday dinner. When the doorbell rang at seven that evening, Mom put on her bathrobe and walked to the living room to greet four couples who arrived with a cake, friends for the past quarter century. She sat in the recliner facing the river, and we gathered in a circle of chairs around her. The pumpkins glowed, the candles burned, the eyes of twenty loving souls filled the room with warmth and light as we sang birthday greetings to my father. Mom made jokes, remembered past gifts, and laughed with her family and friends; she even ate a piece of homemade German chocolate cake with ice cream. We were all astounded by her strength and presence of mind during the party, and touched by the love that seemed to transcend her pain—a beautiful evening for all of us. After the guests left, she sat in the chair for another hour and then asked for help back to her room.

The next morning I rose early to stuff a turkey for our Thanksgiving dinner. Mom woke late and refused her medicine, saying she needed to use the bathroom first. My sister and I supported her on both sides and walked her to the seat, but when we tried to help her back to bed, she said, "No!" and sat down each time we stood her up.

Judy went for help, and I fell to my knees to hold Mom so she wouldn't fall. She wrapped her arms around my neck, pulled me close, and held me so tightly I couldn't move, could hardly breathe. What a strange sight we must have been, mother and daughter holding each other over a toilet seat. Finally, with additional help, we lifted Mom to a kitchen chair and carried her like firemen back to the hospital bed. From that moment on she refused all food and water and pills. We finally dissolved morphine in a spoon and convinced her to swallow it, but she was done trying to live; the death watch had officially begun.

The first realization of her will to die was the hardest: My father cried when he understood that she would not leave the bed for turkey dinner; he cried even more when he saw her calendar with a big black circle around October 25th. I rubbed her feet and listened to a CD of the old hymns she loved so much: "Father, we come to thee," sang the tenor as a ray of sunshine highlighted the pink rose atop my son's gift.

We took turns sitting with Mom, holding her hand, and shedding the inevitable tears—first one, then the next. We also laughed, remembering our shared history and teasing each other as only the intimate can. I felt tremendous gratitude for the beauty, Harry; the beauty of music and flowers and family sustained me.

The house filled with the smell of roasting turkey even though it was not yet Halloween. My brother arrived at four in the afternoon, carrying broccoli and pies, and the immediate family was finally complete. We frantically searched for the turkey platter to no avail, quickly set a primitive table, and fed the children first. The adults served from the stove—Mom would never have stood for an informal turkey dinner, but we were on our own; the clan was gathered around a holiday feast for the first time in many years, and we tried to cope as best we could.

Keith and I volunteered to give Mom a suppository of pills

so she would sleep during the night without pain. I rolled her over and held her, trying to explain away the indignity of our task. She looked into my eyes and spoke her first clear words since the morning: "No! Please don't." I was shaken and walked outside to regain my composure after we completed our difficult task. The moon was full, a vision come to life, and I found strength within. I could actually feel ethereal threads of pure love wrap around my heart, holding me together.

Mom slept through the night but woke Sunday morning moaning and writhing in pain. We mixed morphine as fast as we could and tried to open her clenched teeth with pleading words. Her angry set of jaw made me think she was mad at me for violating her dignity the night before, but I had no choice. We fed her morphine throughout the day and positioned the bedpan against her will.

Sunday afternoon the grandchildren began to leave, each saying, "Good-bye, Grandma," each leaving with some form of "I love you" spoken through slow and heavy lips. A few friends arrived to see Mom, and she managed to squeeze a hand or two. She seemed to rouse for the first greetings and the last good-byes, and to protest the indignities.

When Aunt Ivy helped with a sponge bath, we heard Mom say very clearly to her sister, "Don't let me go like this." My brother, wishing for one lucid minute, said he would end it all if only she could ask. Mom struggled for breath and mumbled the same word whenever we touched her: "No." We had no choice. We changed soiled sheets and reluctantly decided to use an adult diaper while tears formed in the corner of Mom's eyes and fell down her pale cheeks; she had no choice.

During the night I heard her moan and hurried to mix the morphine. Like a nurse, I decided on two capsules and spooned them quickly while stroking her head. I told her I loved her and heard—as clear as a bell—"I love you too, sweetie." Forgiveness filled the void that was starting to form in the center of my being, filled the heart of the child that resides within; her words filled me with peace. They were the last words I heard her speak.

By Monday morning, Mom's three children—my brother, my sister, myself—had formed an efficient team. We had no leader and no agenda other than caring for her. We met on the deck, discussing how much morphine to use, when to change the sheets, how to say good-bye. Dad talked of cremation and the memorial service, of tax status and insurance rates; he took his mind where his heart refused to go, but the siblings urged her to reach for the light, to let go of her life, to trust the care of her seven grandchildren and grieving husband to us. We encouraged each other to speak the final words of gratitude and love, to share unspoken truth, to give personal last rites to our dying mother.

After a while, we wondered if she was holding on to make

peace with Dad. He worked nonstop around the house—finding blankets, washing towels, tending to the mechanics of our care—but saying good-bye was almost beyond his strength. The siblings each spent time alone with Mom behind a closed door, and my father finally took his turn late in the evening. Besides the rattle in her chest, the tears that rolled down her cheeks were the only signs of life. I threw together a soup from leftover turkey and the fresh noodles Michael brought for Dad's birthday present, the ones he made with our new pasta machine. Mom's heart raced; her limbs were swollen and cold.

We held a rotating vigil throughout the night and roused the next sibling with cups of hot tea at the end of each shift. Judy, my sentimental sister, took the first watch. "I don't do death well," she admits through flowing tears, but she refused to leave Mom's side until after 2 A.M. She spoke to Mom of life and death and asked her to say hello to Karen—the friend she lost nineteen years before.

Don sat with Mom until four-thirty and then woke me with a steaming cup. "She panics when she can't breathe," he says. "Just talk to her in a calm voice. It seems to help." My stoic brother, the one who guards his emotions closely, gave his mother all she needed—soothing words of comfort on a dark night. My dad came upstairs around seven-thirty, looking haggard—beyond old—and said he had been listening to the monitor all night in his basement bedroom, his own private vigil.

We gathered here and there around the house to comfort one another and talk of Mom's unconditional love. This was Mom's final gift: Our family was rising to the challenge. When the hospice team arrived to bathe her, they told us the end was near. We paced the floor with teacups, raised our eyebrows in passing, and echoed the news.

"Soon," we solemnly said one to the other—seasoned veterans of the death watch after three intense days. "Her breathing is changing again."

When the nurses finished, we gathered in the "delivery room" to witness the birth of our mother's soul; she was barely hanging on between rattling breaths. We shed tears and held our breath through every long pause: ten seconds, a ragged breath; twenty seconds, a ragged breath; thirty seconds....Dad placed his hand over her heart and pushed several times. "Come on, Marian!" he cried. She gasped once more, and then my father felt the heart of the woman he has lived with and loved for forty-four years beat for the final time. I looked at the bedroom clock: Mom departed with the angels at 11 A.M., October 29, 1996.

Dad's first words, through sobs, were: "Put her in something nice. I don't want her to be seen this way." I turned to the closet and pulled out the rose-covered shirt she liked so well and wore for the first time at Wildhorse Casino; the angel pin I bought for her at Cape Foulweather was attached over the left breast.

Hospice nurses dressed her body, and soon the house was filled with people. I wandered into the bedroom a dozen times to look at her peaceful face; never before had I seen a dead body and finally understood the reason for an open casket. As I sat by the bed, her hand seemed to twitch; then a few minutes later a flower over her heart rose slightly, like a ghost breath. During the past seven months I have watched her sleep so often, my mind created movement where there was no longer life. I stroked her head, held her cold hand, and finally moved the angel pin from her shirt to mine—Dad did not want the pin to burn with her body.

The immediate family gathered for a final prayer—three siblings and both parents holding hands by candlelight—and spoke words of gratitude for the woman with whom we have shared our life. I gave thanks for the lessons of forgiveness and unconditional love I will hopefully always remember to live. At 5 P.M. we transferred her body to the gurney, and placed a rose from Karen's mother's garden upon her breast before the maroon bag was zipped closed.

I believe that in the end, after life and death, angels wrap themselves around the sleeping survivor and transport mind, soul, and personality to the heavenly world, where they wake surrounded by celestial beings of pure love. Survivors rise from the ashes of earthly existence in a new body formed of strength and beauty, on a new world filled with adventure and truth, with a new life designed for learning and love; they rise filled with the profound joy of knowing they have survived with their identity intact. This is the glory of the resurrection morning when life begins anew, when the lost beloved gather and speak of wonders, when faith becomes reality. This is the first step in my mother's journey to the I AM, the first awakening of her true self in spiritual form, the first chance for Mom to rise and flower in the perfect soil of a blameless world. My prayers are with her.

There is so much more to tell, Harry, but I will wait for another day. I send gratitude for your friendship, and for the letters—they mean more to me now, as you can well imagine.

With love,

Janet

NOVEMBER 6, 1996

The Dalles/Angelkeep

Dear Harry,

Mornings are hard for my father just like they were for my mother. After Mom's death he continued to rise with the sun to "fix her pills" as he has done every day for two years, but eventually he remembered she was gone before he reached the kitchen cupboard where he kept her medicine; now he remembers before he moves from bed, and by the time he stands near the coffeepot on the kitchen counter, his eyes are red from crying. "I've become so sentimental in my old age," he explains, and wipes the tears that threaten to fall.

Because he wanted all her personal belongings out of the house as soon as possible, we bagged up the contents of closets and drawers and took them to the Salvation Army in Keith's dented pickup just two days after her death. Mom's lifetime collection of clothes filled eight plastic lawn bags and three cardboard boxes; they were exchanged for a paper receipt. Judy and I kept a few sweatshirts and nightgowns, but most everything Mom owned was white with a splash of blue or pink—she was the queen of coordinates—and I usually wear black and denim, so everything went in the bag, even the two jackets I bought for her last May. Perhaps I should have kept one for my own sentimental old age, but a transient stoicism prevailed.

Dad asked me to write Mom's obituary. I intended to write a tribute to her, highlighting the love and friendship she became known for in a dozen circles; I managed to fill out the form provided, listing names of family members and dates of events, vital statistics that tell you when and where a person lived but little of how and why. The local paper printed the wrong date for the memorial service, so they ran the obituary two days in a row, including every piece of information provided on the form as an apology the second time.

I was struck by a complete paragraph consisting of four simple words: She was a homemaker. When I filled out the form, this seemed such an unfair way to describe a lifetime of work, but when I saw the words in print, I knew she would consider these four words a tribute and they were.

During the death watch Pastor Jim talked with us about Mom's funeral. He envisioned the standard sanctuary service with a reception to follow, but this was not her wish. She wanted a party, a celebration of life, a gathering of friends and family complete with music, flowers, food, and conversation, which is how I described it in her obituary. She considered funerals barbaric, as you may recall, and talked at length about her wishes. When she learned of her terminal illness seven months ago, she even asked a professional singer she had grown to love if he would perform at the celebration and he agreed, although after her death we did not expect him to travel a thousand miles to sing for her.

The four days between her death and the celebration were a whirlwind of activity: We reserved the community room at the church, arranged for a light meal of sandwiches and salads, bought out the floral department at Safeway, and helped my brother make a tape of Mom's favorite songs. He set up the recording equipment in the basement, gathered all her CDs and tapes, and asked Judy and me to approve the final selections. When I told him she liked the Beach Boys, he was dumbfounded, but I remembered several occasions when Mom played "Help Me Rhonda" at full volume to reflect the intensity of her anger. Don found a few Beach Boys CDs and selected an upbeat song to play after the gospel hymns.

Two days before the celebration Mom's beloved singer called to say he couldn't break his promise to her and would fly from Phoenix for the event. My father was both overwhelmed and surprised that everything seemed to be turning out just as Mom had planned.

When we arrived at the church—a bit late because Dad scalped his head on a board in the basement—there was a sign on the door that said MARIAN'S PARTY. Inside the community room were twenty round tables, each decorated with a vase of bright flowers; a buffet service along the side wall; and a small shrine onstage with a picture of Mom and Dad bordered by two burning candles. Every table was filled with friends and family, some sitting and talking, some with tears rolling down their faces. Don's tape played in the background, which proved to be the grandchildren's undoing.

Throughout the long illness—the slow deterioration of their grandmother's body and the final traumatic end—the children held their emotions in check, crying a few stray tears in the arms of a parent, but mostly watching the entire process of her mortal demise with a sense of wonder, it seemed. But emotion spilled from the children as they sat around the table in their best clothes, listened to their grandmother's favorite music, and remembered the woman who somehow managed to make each one feel special.

Pastor Jim, serving as master of ceremonies, remarked that Marian always got her way, as evidenced by such a unique gathering, and invited the hundred or so in attendance to eat, drink, and share memories of her life. I wandered around the room and tried to match faces with names. Like an ambassador for my mother, I greeted as many friends and family as I could, always grateful when old friends reintroduced themselves first. My father later told me that he had somehow managed to remember everyone's name for the first time in his life; a remarkable feat considering the state of his mind, and his head.

The singer, David, waited until the buffet line dwindled and then started the show. He walked around the room with a wireless microphone and made eye contact with every friend and family member while he sang Mom's favorite songs. Then he offered the microphone to anyone who wanted to share a memory of Marian. We heard stories of compassion and endless support, of understanding and forgiveness, of unconditional love. Two dozen people with nervous voices raised their hands to speak, and when they finished, a more complete picture of my mother emerged than the one I've been holding for forty years.

Many of Mom's friends confirmed the theme Pastor Jim started: Marian always got her way. It seems that in the getting of her way Mom convinced people to take trips they would never have taken, to attend special events that first sounded dull, to make friends with the awkward and unusual, to forgive mistakes and love each another. Everyone in the room, we learned later, had received flowers or a card of encouragement from Mom during some difficult time.

David sang a few more emotional songs, Pastor Jim said a prayer, and the party was suddenly over—too soon for most family members. We packed up the extra food, gave away the flowers, cleaned the kitchen, and went home.

The next day a friend of Pastor Jim's stopped by my father's house and shared a moving story: After the party the pastor went home and told of the evening's events. Without warning he was overcome with emotion and cried for some time in his wife's arms, an unusual response from a man of faith who has buried dozens of parishioners. Perhaps a more complete picture emerged of the troubled woman he had counseled for twenty-five years; perhaps he was unprepared for the emotional impact of her unique celebration. Another friend called to say his parents had been so impressed with Mom's party, they had changed their minds about memorial services. Mom would have been pleased.

The following week Judy and I continued to discard and occasionally claim Mom's personal belongings. We found a large box filled with cards and letters, and Judy convinced me to help sort them; Mom had once joked that this task would be repayment for past sins. She was right. Every letter and card I had sent to her since the age of twelve had been saved in that box; every business card, advertising plan, and job evaluation I had shared with my parents over the years found its way into my surprised hands twenty years later.

Memories of my life flooded through my mind like a river of dreams, remembered in segments after a long and restless night. I must have thanked her for understanding a hundred times; for her support and love, another hundred. Only one letter revealed a misunderstanding, a rite of passage for a twenty-something who had chosen to leave a seemingly stable relationship in search of adventure and fame—against a mother's advice.

Judy and I made separate stacks for the immediate family and gave the remaining notes and cards to Dad for disposal. There were more than a thousand cards from family and friends thanking Mom for various gifts and loving support. As I looked at each card, the words of those who gathered to celebrate her life rang in my ears. I put my memories in a clear plastic bag and carried them to Angelkeep.

My homecoming back at the cabin was sweet: Keith and the children had prepared a special meal complete with candles and wine. While sitting at the table surrounded by my loved ones, I was reminded that saying good-bye for the final time was an undeniable aspect of family life. In order to help my children prepare, I pledged to smile through the inevitable tears in the weeks and months to come.

With gratitude and love,

Janet

NOVEMBER 21, 1996

Angelkeep

Dear Harry,

When my mother was eleven years old and a new student at the elementary school in Portland—transferred from Montana to Oregon because of death and poverty—she received a gift from another student in their annual Christmas exchange. The boy who gave her the little ceramic statue of Joseph could not have known how significant his gift would become; could not have known that his classmate would keep the statue on her bedroom dresser for the next fifty-eight years; could not have known that three weeks before she died of cancer the statue would pass from her hands to those of her forty-year-old daughter, a gift with exceptional meaning.

I imagine my excited mother unwrapping the small package while sitting at her wooden school desk, wondering whether a treasure or some thoughtless trinket lay inside, finding the hand-made image of Jesus' father wrapped in white tissue, feeling a spontaneous bond with the small figurine: Joseph also died before his time, leaving young children behind.

But the significance of the statue had more to do with Mom's sense of worthiness to receive such a gift, I believe, than with the story of Joseph's life. The gift embodied a sense of belonging despite worn-out clothes and a chaotic family life; the gift connected a deeply wounded child with the message of love and forgiveness embraced by the Christian traditions. I imagine my lonely mother cradling the five-inch painted statue with her delicate hands, stroking the long folds of Joseph's cloak with gentle fingers, placing the gift in a prominent position atop the old dresser she shared with her three sisters. She must have defended the fragile icon fiercely, denying her siblings access, guarding it with every breath. How else to explain the longevity of a hollow piece of thin ceramic that survived my mother's life in the flesh, a life punctuated by transition and trauma?

I imagine the statue being carefully wrapped in newspaper a dozen times, moved from home to home in a cardboard box, unwrapped before her other possessions, placed on every successive bedroom dresser, and greeted each morning as she reached for her clothes—a silent witness and immutable bridge between where she had been and where she was going.

Joseph, with the green turban and silver gown, adorned the dresser in her stepmother's home during Mom's difficult teenage years; Joseph, with black beard and bowed head, traveled with Mom to the many apartments she shared with girlfriends over the next ten years; Joseph, with folded hands and slightly bent knee, moved with Mom when she married my father, and lived on their dresser for forty-four years.

I imagine scenes from her life with the statue included: The nights she slept with a newborn child cradled in her arms; the mornings she rose and dressed alone while her husband worked out of town; the evenings she lay in bed with him and worried aloud for one of her kin; the afternoons she spent grooming herself for the special occasions all families share—the confirmations, the graduations, the weddings. And I imagine Joseph a witness to every traumatic scene when Mom lost her way: every hurried packing when she fled the house, every pleading glance from her worried children, every silent return to a bedroom unchanged.

I remember standing in her various bedrooms as a child,

looking at the statue of Joseph and wanting to hold him; over the years I grew more enamored of the treasure my mother would not let us touch. Even when Mom was gone Joseph remained, watching and waiting for the return of the child-woman to whom he belonged, holding her place in the family. As long as Joseph continued to stand with bowed head and folded hands on top of Mom's dresser, I felt certain she would return, would once again wake and dress in the bedroom where her treasure stood guard; he was still there three weeks ago when I found the courage to ask for him, the only trinket on the cherry-wood surface of her current bedroom dresser.

We were making a list of gifts for my brother and sister, writing in a red notebook the various household items Mom wanted to leave her loved ones. "Is there something you want?" she asked while lying in the water bed. I hesitated for a moment, looking to the dresser. "Has anyone mentioned the statue of Joseph?" I quietly said, wondering if she had already promised her oldest possession to someone else.

"Joseph?" she sounded surprised.

"The one that's been on your dresser since you were eleven, Mom," I felt the need to rationalize my request. "Hasn't anyone asked for the statue? Perhaps we should leave him for Dad," I said, unwilling to compete for the sentimental. Mom assured me that no one had asked for him, that he was mine if I wanted him. I did.

"Why don't you take the Joseph statue before you leave today, honey, just to be sure." While Mom was in the bathtub, I carefully wrapped my delicate treasure in a nightshirt for the long trip home.

The statue of Joseph now sitting above our woodstove with the angels is the most tangible memory I have of my mother's life. With my every glance I feel her presence, with every gentle holding of this worn ceramic icon an image comes to life: the image of a traumatic loss slowly transformed by an evolution of love. The Joseph statue embodies the dreams and desires of a lonely child who treasured a gift of friendship for fifty-eight years, embodies the gift of friendship this same child-woman offered to hundreds of others during a lifetime of suffering and love.

Keith and I and the children plan to spend Thanksgiving with friends. We will serve each other from a beautiful platter while sitting together and counting our blessings under the soft glow of candlelight. And I'll remember with gratitude the previous feast when we served ourselves from the roasting pan during the chaotic time of my mother's death. We were thankful then, and we're thankful now for the living truth found in our human lives.

With love to you, my friend,

Janet

D ECEMBER 3, 1996

Angelkeep

Dear Harry,

Several months ago, after my dream of the full moon, I prayed for understanding: What did my spectacular dream-vision mean? While I sat quietly wondering, twin moons appeared in the darkness behind my closed eyes. Two moons, glowing white, emerged, and then moved slowly together until they formed one full moon—larger, brighter, more dynamic than the two that had merged; the moon from my mysterious dream.

After a few seconds the unified moon disappeared, but the vision remained firmly embedded in memory, a revelation both personal and profound. The merging of the moons became a metaphor for my life—for every relationship between myself and others, for every evolution from the unknown to the known, for every fair-minded embrace of another side. The full moon symbolized the strength of duality—of partnership, of perspective, of parts becoming whole in the fullness of time.

The beauty of this image transforms my sorrow. The full moon rises red above the distant hills, travels pink through a silhouette of trees, and shines brilliant white across the vast starscape—an evolving light in the night sky, a window to the soul of my true self. The full moon calls to me from beyond the challenge of my earthly existence, calls to me from the strength of my potential, "Remember who we are, child; remember where we are going." I transcend the parts and become more than the sum; I embrace beauty and discover truth.

The metaphor of the merging moons reminds me of Mom. As I quietly grieve her loss, I gain a greater understanding of her role as my mother—the influence of her history in the formation of my character and the integration of her legacy in the progress of my life; a merging of origin with destiny. The strengths and weaknesses of the woman through whom I entered this world have become parts of my whole.

I recognize her fear in my quickness to ride a wave of impatience or build a wall of anger; I recognize her love in my eagerness to forgive the occasional pain caused by family and friends. These parts have been gently integrated into my being over the course of a lifetime. They have been tempered by an endowment of common sense from my father, transformed by a childhood free from death and poverty, transcended by my growing faith in a spiritual destiny. I have been fortunate. My mother carried these diverse parts in two distinct sides of herself, sides perpetually separated by a childhood trauma that stood like an invisible barrier through the center of her being, a separation so fundamental that healing through integration was impossible for her. Until now.

Death and resurrection have merged the parts of my mortal mother into an eternal whole: child with woman, human with divine. I imagine her two distinct sides—fear and love—moving like two moons toward each other, merging at the moment of death, becoming something new. I imagine her fear dissolved by this union, displaced by the joy of survival, destroyed by the fire of transformation just like her mortal form. And I imagine Mom rising from the ashes with a new form that perfectly reflects the depth of her love, a mirror image of her beautiful soul—a full moon.

The metaphor of the merging moons comes to life every twenty-nine or thirty days, when a brilliant vision hangs in the night sky and reminds me that we are all much more than the sum of our parts—we are evolving spiritual beings in material form, moving toward integration in steps. My journey unfolds this side of the moon, but my mother travels beyond its brilliant reflection; my mother walks and talks with the angels. Someday this door will open for me. Someday I will merge with the side of myself reflected by the light of the full moon, a brilliant and beautiful light that speaks to me in the quiet of my mind: "Breathe deeply, child, for I reside within even now." We merge in small steps, slowly but surely, the human with the divine.

Moonlight shines upon the foot of fresh snow that covers

the ground, casting trees in dark shadow; holiday lights dance around our little cabin, offering warm comfort on a cold night; smoke from the woodstove gently curls and drifts up the mountainside while streams sing at my feet. Life is good, Harry, for both my mother and for me.

And for you? I hear you are soaking up sun in Hawaii. Won't say I'm jealous, but the mornings around here are rather chilly. Hope the world is wonderfully warm wherever you are, my friend.

Much love,

Janet

[EPILOGUE]

hree months have passed since the death of my mother—it is now the winter of her demise. I no longer write letters to Harry, no longer drive to my childhood home, no longer reach for Mom over the phone line. It is the season for grieving.

High peaks are dressed in heavy snow, dark woods stretch like a full bodice across the mountainside, hay fields sleep beneath a white velvet skirt that covers the entire valley. The winter world is stilled by the absence of warmth and light, slowed by the need to conserve strength, silenced by the retreat of warm-blooded beings to burrows and bedrooms; the winter world turns inward for comfort.

It is not as unpleasant as I had imagined, this grieving. I do not feel hurt by the loss of my mother, do not hunger for her voice or her presence, do not languish in memories of our life together. It is also true that tears fall without warning, an overflow of emotion that builds unnoticed in my busy life, an expression of grief that cannot be denied; sudden, mysterious, profound emotion that takes me by complete surprise. Sometimes I smile through these spontaneous tears because I feel an embrace in the midst of such pain—a brief and merciful merging of my own dual natures, the human with the divine.

When I think of the woman to whom I was born, my mind quickly shifts to a cosmic perspective. I have ceased looking back to the pain of her mortal life, refused to dwell upon the shores of her suffering. The vision I hold of her new life grows more vivid with each passing day—a panorama of gentle lands, beautiful beings, and infinite love; the vision I hold transforms my pain.

During the seasons of my mother's demise I learned these comforting truths: Dying without fear requires a mindful embrace of eternity; strength results from both suffering and love; faith will temper my grief. During the seasons I evolved a few steps beyond fear, and for this I will always be grateful.

Janet Farrington Graham

February 4, 1997

[ACKNOWLEDGMENTS]

Partnership is one of the fundamental objectives of my life. Whether with family or friends, teachers or students, the seen or the unseen, working in creative relationships defines my reality.

And so, I would like to thank my partners. First, of course, are my parents, Howard and Marian, who committed the full measure of their resources to my upbringing. And my brother and sister, Don and Judy, who shared and competed with me for those same resources, strengthening both my will and my identity. And all the aunts and uncles, cousins and stepcousins, who defined my first community. I remember our gatherings with joy.

Second, I would like to thank the partners in my spiritual community. Harry McMullan and Steve Dreier you know from the book, and so understand firsthand the incomparable beauty of our friendship, without which there would have been no book. Behind the scenes there are others—Jennifer and Mo Siegel, who became my champions; Alison Gardner, Marcy Hamilton, and Starla Dubois, who were my first readers and best fans; and all my coworkers at The Urantia Book Fellowship, where we struggle to unfold a revelation together, and grow by leaps and bounds.

I often wondered why authors thank their editors so profusely at this point, and now I know. Kate Hartson, my editor, could see into the soul of this work, untying knots and highlighting potential with an ink pen and a small stack of Post-it notes. Jennie Halfant was my touchstone, providing a novice with the details, the whens and hows of birthing a book. And Terry Newell, the publisher, took a chance on an unusual manuscript and forged new ground for Time Life. I would also like to thank Marc Jaffe, who provided my very first breath of hope.

Finally, I would like to thank my husband, Keith, for his vision of a mountain homestead, and for his belief in my dream. And I would like to thank our three children, Michael, Rachel, and Hannah, with whom we share a beautiful life on the edge of the Oregon wilderness. This book was written at a desk in the middle of our small cabin, so my children learned to walk and talk quietly during the many hours I was rooted at the keys. You three are my greatest treasures, and I love you infinity squared.